STOP DATING RED FLAGS

Hilariously Honest Lessons on Love, Lies & Learning to Trust Yourself

Karen A. Dahlman

STOP DATING RED FLAGS

Hilariously Honest Lessons on Love, Lies & Learning to Trust Yourself

Published by
Creative Visions Publications
PO Box 25246
Scottsdale, AZ 85255
United States of America
creativevisionspublications.com

Publication Date: March, 2026
ISBN: 979-8-9877838-2-5

Cover Design & Cover Artwork by Karen A. Dahlman

Disclaimer
This book is based on the author's true personal experiences. Names and certain identifying details of individuals have been changed to protect privacy. Events are presented from the author's perspective and memory, and some details may be simplified or condensed for clarity and narrative flow.

This book reflects the author's personal opinions, perceptions, and interpretations of events and is intended for educational and reflective purposes. It is not intended as professional, medical, or therapeutic advice. Any resemblance to actual persons, living or dead, is coincidental.

Dedication

To every woman who has silenced her gut, ignored the red flags, or stayed too long hoping he would change. This one is for you.

To my girlfriends who handed me wine, wigs, and tough love when I needed it most. To the wrong men, I thank you for the lessons, the material, and the entertainment.

Without all of you, I would not be here laughing, wiser, and walking like the Queen I was always meant to be.

STOP DATING RED FLAGS

Hilariously Honest Lessons on Love, Lies & Learning to Trust Yourself

Table of Contents

SECTION II: The Pretenders & Performers – Men Who Played a Role

DAMIAN – THE MUSIC MAN WHO PLAYED DOCTOR

LANCE – THE CABANA BOY

SECTION III: The Gross-Out Files – When Red Flags Turn Cringe

Preface

If you are holding this book, chances are you have survived at least a few dating disasters, or at a minimum a couple of "what the actual hell was I thinking?" moments.

Let me just say this right up front. I have been there.

I am not writing this as some flawless woman perched on a mountain of perfect decisions, sipping champagne with her equally perfect soulmate. No, I am writing this as a woman who lived it:

The charming liars whose stories were so good, I wanted to believe them.
The "fun" guys who turned out to be walking bundles of red flags.
The ones who needed fixing, and I thought I was the one to do it.
The cute ones who slowly made me feel gross just being around them.
Yes, even the so-called "successful" ones who turned out to be scammers in suits.

I have dated almost every archetype of the wrong man, from Cowboy Con Artists to Trailer Park Charmers, Married Millionaires, Broken Athletes, and the unforgettable Human Ashtray.

Every time, I thought, *This one will be different.*
Every time, my gut whispered, *No, he will not.*
Every time, I ignored it until I finally could not anymore.

Why Listen to Me?

Because I have made the mistakes you are probably making or are about to make.

I have stayed too long. I have given too much. I have excused too many "icks." I have second-guessed myself more than I care to admit.

Here is what I learned: you do not have to keep doing that.

It is about learning to recognize red flags the moment they appear, not months or years down the road.
It is about trusting yourself deeply enough that you do not need to "see where it goes" with someone who is clearly not your match.
It is about getting brutally honest with yourself about what you are tolerating and why.

What This Book IS NOT

It is not a fluffy guide about manifesting the perfect man.
It is not a bitter rant about how all men are trash.
It is definitely not written by someone pretending to have the perfect relationship.

What I do have are decades of lived experience, mistakes, hard-won wisdom, and a psychotherapist's insight into why we fall into these patterns and how to break them.

What This Book IS

It is part memoir, part girlfriend-style intervention, and part no-nonsense guide. It is honest, funny, sometimes a little raw, and sprinkled with enough sass to keep it real.

It is the conversation you wish you could have over wine with your smartest, most brutally honest friend who loves you enough to tell you the truth.

Why I REALLY Wrote This

I do not want you or any woman to waste years doubting yourself, second-guessing your intuition, or believing you have to "fix" someone to make them love you. I want you to see the red flags for what they are.

They are not mysteries. They are information:

Blurred boundaries
Habits that make your gut say "ick"
Stories that do not add up
Men who need a mother, not a partner
Men who want access, not intimacy

Most importantly, I want you to see that you are not "too picky," "too much," or "too hard to love." You are learning to trust yourself.

So, buckle up. I am about to introduce you to all the archetypes I dated so you can spot them a mile away.

By the time you finish this book, you will have:

A radar for red flags you cannot ignore
The confidence to walk away without guilt or overthinking
The ability to trust your own gut like your life depends on it, because in love, it does

Welcome to ***Stop Dating Red Flags***.

It is time to stop wasting your time, stop doubting your instincts, and finally trust yourself. This is not just about the men. It is about you, your patterns, and, most importantly, the path back to yourself.

Introduction

This book exists because women deserve to laugh, learn, and finally trust themselves before wasting another second on the wrong men.

Teaser: "Consider this your permission slip to stop blaming yourself for missing red flags and start spotting them in record time."

This Is Not Just Another Dating Disaster Book

If you are holding this book, I already know a few things about you:

You are smart, but maybe you have still fallen for charm.
You are strong, but you have carried more than your share.
You are hopeful, and hope can blur red flags into potential.

Sound familiar? Then you are in the right place.

This book is not about bashing men. It is about spotting patterns, laughing at the ridiculousness, and reclaiming your crown before you decide who gets access to it.

You are going to meet some real characters in these pages—men who lied, charmed, manipulated, or just flat-out grossed me out. Some of their antics will make you laugh out loud. Others will make you cringe and whisper, "Oh hell, I dated that guy too."

However, this is not just about the men. It is about what happens when we silence our intuition, override our gut, and trade our worth for the hope of being loved.

You will laugh at my stories. You will see your own patterns in them. By the end, you will know how to stop repeating the same mistakes and start dating with clarity, confidence, and a whole lot more self-respect.

This Book Is Part Cautionary Tale, Part Self-love Manifesto

It will entertain you. It might sting. It will definitely remind you that you deserve more than half-truths, crumbs, or chaos.

Are you ready to cringe a little, laugh a lot, and maybe heal? Are you ready to finally stop auditioning for a man's love and start seeing if he is even worthy of yours?

Good.

Let us begin.

STOP DATING RED FLAGS

Hilariously Honest Lessons on Love, Lies & Learning to Trust Yourself

KAREN A. DAHLMAN

SECTION I: The First Red Flags – The Foundation of the Pattern

Before I could spot a red flag, I was too busy falling for the Cowboy Con Artists. They were the rugged charmers with boots, lies, and convincing smiles. They were not riding into the sunset; they were riding on my hope that they were who they claimed to be. Clay and Colt laid the blueprint for my patterns. They showed me how easily fantasy hides reality and how ignoring my gut only delays heartbreak.

Teaser: "He was not a cowboy; he was a con in boots."

Clay – The Starter Liar
Colt – The Texas Sequel & Marriage Nightmare

2

Clay – The Starter Liar

(aka: The Boot-Wearing Heart Breaker)

Clay was my first dip into trouble, disguised as "safe."

I was twenty-three, knee-deep in graduate school, exhausted and overworked. When Clay appeared, he felt like a lifeline. He knew a mutual friend from college and was staying at that friend's house. *Oh, he's connected,* I thought. *He must be trustworthy.*

Spoiler: he was not.

The Original Cowboy Con

Clay had a way of making his life sound impressive. He claimed his mother had passed away and left him a construction company in Florida that he needed to "manage." It sounded noble.

Reality? His mother was alive and well, remarried, and living in a trailer park with her new husband. No construction company. No inheritance. Just a story designed to hook me.

He also pretended to have a job. Every morning, he left my apartment as if he was heading to work. In reality, he wandered around town aimlessly while I busted my ass in graduate school.

The weirdest thing? He "accidentally" let my indoor cat outside. When I asked how that was even possible, he shrugged and said,

"Oh, maybe the cat jumped off the balcony."

Right. Cats do not survive random balcony jumps from two stories up.

If I did not let the cat out, the only other person entering and leaving my apartment was Clay. My cat did not know how to turn a doorknob.

He was careless. Then he lied about it. My cat returned later, unharmed, with better instincts than the man I was dating.

Like other men after him, Clay had nowhere to go, so he moved into my place. I did not even tell my parents. Deep down, I knew it would not sound right.

Still, I stayed.

I was young. I wanted to believe the fantasy over the facts. I thought, *Maybe he just needs someone to believe in him.*

What I Should Have Noticed

A man who starts with small lies rarely stops there.
If someone's story feels too polished or too pitiful, it is probably fiction.
A grown man pretending to go to work is not building a life; he is building a lie.
If you feel the need to hide him from your parents, that is not love. It is your gut waving a giant red flag.

Takeaway

If a man's backstory sounds too tragic and too noble, double-check it.
Just because someone knows a mutual friend does not make them safe.
A guy who cannot keep his own life together will eventually try to live in yours.

Lesson

Clay taught me that you cannot build a future with a man who does not even have a present.

Red Flags to Remember

He left for "work" with nothing to show for it.
His stories were long on drama but short on proof.
He blamed accidents, like losing my cat, on anything but himself.

Mic-Drop Truth

The first liar does not just waste your time. He trains you to normalize deception.

Colt – The Texas Sequel & Marriage Nightmare

(aka: The Cowboy Con Artist 2.0)

Colt looked like the upgrade. He was tall, rugged, charming, with that easy Texas drawl and polished "big plans." I met him at twenty-eight, at that vulnerable point in life where everyone around me was settling down, getting married, or already knee-deep in family life.

I thought, *Well, maybe it is my turn.*

I did not know I was about to step into the longest, most gut-wrenching Western drama of my life, complete with lies, betrayal, and the kind of heartbreak that makes you question everything you thought you knew about yourself.

The Perfect Engagement at First

At the beginning, Colt seemed different. He was attentive, fun, and painted this incredible picture of our future together. We dated for a year, got engaged, and he moved into my home when his lease ended.

Here is what I did not know then, but learned much later:

He had been married twice already. According to him, both ex-wives were "crazy" and "ruined his life."
He never earned the law degree he bragged about. It was all a lie.
He had a criminal history of embezzlement that would later land him in jail.

I uncovered all of it slowly, piece by ugly piece, when the cracks in the mask started to show.

The Lies, Lies, Lies

Colt's life was one long, polished story designed to keep me, and everyone else, hooked.

He said he was some high-level executive at a major Texas company. Reality? He was embezzling money.

He told me his marriages ended because the women were unstable. Reality? He was the chaos.

He told me he was "building a future with me." Reality? He was robbing Peter to pay Paul and using my stability as his soft landing.

The biggest lie was his life itself. If his lips were moving, he was lying.

The Ring That Disappeared

One day, my engagement ring disappeared. In hindsight, this was right before all hell broke loose and I left him.

When I asked where it was, he casually said, "Hmm, maybe it went down the sink?"

I did not believe him. So, I called a plumber and we pulled the U-pipe, but no ring.

His next excuse? "Oh, maybe your cat ate it."

My cat **DID NOT** eat a diamond ring. He took it and pawned it. He lied straight to my face like it was the most reasonable thing in the world.

The Breaking Point

By the time I grasped the depth of his deceit, I was already in the marriage and living the nightmare. I was tied to this slow-motion train wreck, and every day was another red flag I could not unsee.

I would lie in bed at night and cry myself to sleep, feeling trapped in a marriage that was not real. I leaned heavily on my friends just to survive emotionally because I did not think I could endure it alone.

When I finally left, I dug into his past. I did the research he never wanted me to do and found the stack of court documents at the Travis County courthouse in Austin, Texas, exposing everything: the failed marriages, the embezzlement, the jail time, the false education.

All of it was right there in black and white. I just had not looked.

The Western Drama

Being with Colt was like starring in the worst kind of Western:

He came in looking like the hero, riding high on charm and promises, but by the final act, you realize you are not in a love story. You are in a lawless drama, surrounded by the tumbleweeds of lies.

You know what? You cannot save the outlaw.

Why I Stayed

I stayed because a year had passed, and at twenty-nine, I felt vulnerable. I stayed because I thought, *I should probably marry someone by now. This is what people do at this age.*

These men swoop in exactly when you are doubting yourself. When you are craving stability. They sell you a dream you are ready to believe.

How to Spot a Colt

He is charming but vague about his past.
His life sounds impressive, but the details are slippery.
He blames every failed relationship on "crazy" women.
He plays the victim to earn sympathy.
Your gut says something is off, but you override it because you want the dream to be real.

What I Should Have Noticed

When charm feels rehearsed, it probably is.
If every ex is unstable and every story shifts under pressure, something is wrong.
Crying before your wedding is not nerves. It is your intuition screaming through the silence.
When a man rewrites his past to sell you a future, you are not the co-author. You are the mark.

Takeaway

Colt taught me the most painful truth: love does not fix liars, and you are not the final chapter in someone else's tall tale.

Lesson

A man who lies about his past will burn your future alongside his own.
Charm is not character. Consistency is.
If you have to investigate the man you married, your intuition already investigated him first.
Love does not rehabilitate deception. It only postpones the damage.
You cannot build stability on a foundation of secrets.

Red Flags to Remember

He lied about his education, his jobs, even his marriages.

He gaslit me about the ring, the money, and the truth.

He embezzled from his employer and still played the victim.

I ignored my body the night before the wedding.

Mic-Drop Truth

Colt was not just a cowboy con artist; he was the full Western tragedy. I was the leading lady who finally walked off set.

SECTION II: The Pretenders & Performers – Men Who Played a Role

These were the men who put on the best show: musicians with stage presence, "doctors" with polished degrees, businessmen with impressive titles, and confident charmers who knew exactly how to command a room. Their confidence felt real, their stories sounded credible, and their lives appeared solid. They sold me an illusion I wanted to believe.

Each one understood how to perform. They knew which role to step into and how to hold it just long enough to feel convincing. I was not just dating men; I was dating carefully constructed identities. The problem was not that they had flaws. Everyone does. The problem was that I mistook performance for character and charisma for integrity. Yet, the curtain always falls. It just takes time.

Teaser: "They were great actors; just terrible men."

Damian – The Music Man Who Played Doctor
Lance – The Cabana Boy
Maxwell – The Businessman Scammer
Brandy – The Liquor Liar
Johnny – The Outlaw

Damian – The Music Man Who Played Doctor

(aka: Dr. Fake Rockstar MD)

Damian was the kind of man who could impress anyone at first glance. He wore many hats, or so he claimed.

He told me he owned a computer repair company. He told me he was a chiropractor. He told me he was a musician, the lead singer and bass player of a rock band. He even told me he was an author, an "expert" on dating women.

I should have known right then.

The Impressive Resume That Was Not

In the beginning, I saw pieces of his "life" that looked real enough.

He did repair computers. He did play in a band at a small dive called the I-Bar. He even had a little self-help radio presence, and there was a woman—a psychologist no less—who believed everything he said.

That is what made me question myself. She was a psychologist and had him on her radio show. She validated his stories.

So, I thought, *Maybe I am just being too critical. Maybe I need to stop overanalyzing.* What I did not stop to consider was that she might have been drinking the same Kool-Aid.

This woman also lived in a house filled with Barbies. It was, quite literally, a Barbie museum. That should have been a clue right there.

The "Doctor" Title

One day, over lunch, I could not take it anymore. I was holding back this rising fury, this quiet rage, at the audacity of this man.

He had told me before he had a DC, Doctor of Chiropractic. Then it somehow became a PhD.

(I am quietly thinking, *Are you claiming the MD letters next?*)

Here is the thing: I know how hard it is to earn a degree like that. I have done the work. I have written the papers. I have written a thesis. I know what it takes.

So, I finally asked him, point blank: "I do not understand how you say you have a PhD when you told me you had a DC before. Which is it?"

Do you know what he said? "Oh honey, look, of course I do. I went to the University of Phoenix online. Oh, you're just worried about nothing. It is okay."

That was his answer. A casual, "oh honey" like I was just a silly little girl for even questioning him. Meanwhile, he slapped "PhD" after his name and soaked up every moment someone called him "Doctor."

It was insulting, manipulative, and a blatant lie.

The Books & The Misogyny

Oh, and did I mention he wrote books? He wrote a whole series on dating women.

I wish I could tell you the titles, but honestly, I do not want to give him that much credit. Let us just say they were full of bitterness, misogyny, and blame disguised as "advice."

He even had a self-help online column. It was ironic, almost laughable. A man who could not hold a shred of integrity was trying to teach other men how to date women.

It would have been funny if it was not so pathetic.

The Illusion Cracks

Looking back, I see exactly how he kept me hooked in the beginning.

I saw his band play live. I saw him fix a computer. I saw glimpses of things that made his stories believable. He sprinkled just enough truth to sell the lie.

When you see just enough of something, you start filling in the blanks for him. I told myself:

Well, he really does play music, so maybe he really is as talented as he says.
Well, that psychologist believes him, so maybe I am just too skeptical.

No, I was not skeptical enough.

What I Should Have Noticed

When a man lists more job titles than a LinkedIn scammer, that is not ambition. It is bullshit in costume.
If his degrees keep changing and his confidence only shows up when someone calls him "Doctor," **RUN**.
A man who needs applause more than accountability is performing, not partnering.
And if the only thing consistent about him is his ability to deflect, you already have your answer.

Takeaway

If a man's "resume" sounds too good to be true, it probably is. A few sprinkles of truth do not make the whole story real.

Titles mean nothing without integrity behind them.

If he makes you feel silly for questioning him, he has already shown you the truth. He is a liar who thrives on keeping you off balance.

Lesson

If someone needs to constantly tell you how impressive they are, they are not.

If they hide behind fancy titles and vague accomplishments, they are probably lying.

If they make you feel small or silly for questioning them, they are showing you exactly who they are.

Red Flags to Remember

He bragged about being a "doctor" but could not back it up with proof. He wrote books tearing women down while pretending to be an expert. He always had an "oh honey" excuse to deflect accountability.

Mic-Drop Truth

When a man needs to create an entire fantasy to feel important, he is not a mystery. He is just insecure in 4K.

Lance – The Cabana Boy

(aka: The Ego that Needed a Life Vest)

Meet Lance. He was tallish, lean, and undeniably handsome. He was the kind of guy who turned heads when he walked into a room, or more accurately, when he strolled shirtless by the pool.

On the surface, he was fun, charming, the "let's just relax and vibe" kind of guy.

And yes, the rumors were true.

The Medical Anomaly

His dong, and let us be real, there is no delicate way to say this, was legendary.

So much so that when he was born, the doctors were stunned. They actually tracked his "growth" for years like some sort of bizarre case study. Somewhere out there, in an old medical journal, there is probably a write-up titled:

"The Boy with the Anomaly."

Even soft, it was the size of a normal man. Hard? Forget it. That thing had its own ZIP code. You would think a man with that kind of gift would ooze confidence.

But here is the twist…

The Shallow End of the Pool

For all that mythical size, Lance had the confidence of a popped balloon. On the outside, he seemed impressive, flashy even. The second you touched the surface, there was nothing holding it up. All the air just whooshed out.

He owned a pool company in Las Vegas, which in hindsight was the perfect metaphor for his personality: sparkling on the surface, shallow underneath.

When I took him out to a fancy Vegas restaurant, hoping for a romantic, upscale evening, his insecurities started to seep out.

He did not feel like he "belonged" in that kind of space. He fidgeted through dinner, his self-consciousness pouring out in little comments and defensive jokes.

That is when it hit me: this man may have a giant, well, you know, but he could not stay erect in his own life.

The Breakup Flip

After just shy of a year together, I knew I had to end it.

His low self-esteem was suffocating. No amount of reassurance or patience was going to "fix" what was so deeply wired inside him.

But when I finally broke up with him? He flipped the blame. Instead of admitting his lack of confidence was the problem, he accused me of cheating.

There I was, walking away because I could not handle the endless self-doubt, and somehow, I was the villain in his version of the story.

That is classic projection.

The Drawer

There was a moment with Lance that told me everything. There were no raised voices, no blowout fight, and no dramatic confession. The truth came down to a drawer.

He hosted a casual get-together at his place with friends of his and friends of mine. One of my girlfriends was visiting from out of state, so she stayed the night in one of his spare rooms.

No big deal, so I thought.

The next morning, she went into a kitchen drawer looking for a pen. Instead, she found a stack of printed dating profiles: women, photos, and bios. In the drawer, they were not shoved in haphazardly. They were not hidden. They seemed to be curated. Like a low-budget casting call for *The Bachelor: Vegas Pool Edition.*

She woke me up and showed me. What I felt was not confusion. It was clarity.

When Lance finally woke up, I asked him about the drawer, calmly and directly. His first response was not an explanation.

"Why was your friend going through my drawers?" Ah. Interesting pivot. Apparently, the real issue was not the pile of women quietly waiting in his kitchen. It was the audacity of noticing them.

Then came the excuses: they were for a friend, they were old, they were not his, they did not mean anything. Each explanation tripped over the last. What mattered was not which excuse he chose, but how fast the focus shifted. Suddenly, I was the problem. The question was the betrayal. The drawer did not matter.

That is when it clicked. This was not about cheating; it was about hedging, keeping options warm and enjoying the benefits of commitment while quietly shopping for upgrades.

Later, when he accused me of cheating, I almost laughed. The drawer had already told the truth.

What I Should Have Noticed

When a man leads with his looks, or his legendary anatomy, it is often because that is all he has.

If he looks like a Greek god but crumbles at dinner, that is not depth. It is decoration.

No matter how big the package, if the man inside is emotionally small, you will end up carrying the weight.

Takeaway

You cannot fill a man's self-esteem for him. If he does not believe in himself, no amount of love or reassurance will stick. A man who feels "less than" will eventually try to pull you down to his level.

Shallow water looks pretty but will not hold you. Just because something sparkles on the surface does not mean it has substance underneath. Owning a pool company does not mean he knows how to keep his emotional life clean.

Projection is a defense mechanism. When he feels small, he will find a way to make you the problem.

Big is not better. Physical gifts do not replace emotional depth, self-awareness, or confidence.

Lesson

Lance taught me that surface sparkle means nothing without depth.

A man can have the most impressive "package" in the room and still be emotionally bankrupt.

Red Flags to Remember

His confidence was all show; one little fancy dinner was all it took for his insecurities to unravel.

He could not rise to the occasion emotionally, no matter what his anatomy promised.

He tried to flip the script and blame me when I left, projecting his own failings. If he keeps a literal list of "options" while dating, he is not committed. He is hedging.

Mic-Drop Truth

Sure, his anatomy had its own ZIP code, but emotionally, he was barely living past the shallow end of the pool.

Maxwell – The Businessman Scammer

(aka: The "Dear John" of San Diego)

Maxwell was smooth, suave, articulate, and the kind of man who made you feel like you were finally stepping into the kind of story you had always imagined.

He wore confidence like a tailored suit. He walked into a room and women leaned in. He did not just have charm. He had vision: big ideas, big dreams, and big promises.

It started like any other "maybe this is the one" story. We met, sparks flew, and the conversations flowed.

He was the type who quoted visionary leaders, talked about creating legacies, and claimed he was building a company that would change lives. He did not just talk the talk. He looked the part with expensive watches, crisp clothes, the right car, and dinners in places where the maître d' knows your name before you sit down.

I thought, *Finally, a man with sophistication who can actually keep up.*

However, Maxwell was not just walking into my life; he was staging a performance.

The Two-Date Pivot

Here is the craziest part: we only went on two actual dates. Yes, there were only two.

Before I even had a chance to really know him, he seamlessly pivoted the relationship into "business." The flirty texts and romantic dinners faded, replaced with late-night calls about "investment opportunities" and promises of insane returns.

I was not just his date anymore. I became his next business partner.

The Company of Smoke & Mirrors

Maxwell's big "company" was an angel investment firm.

On paper, it looked legit. He had offices. He had staff. He had glossy marketing materials. He even had a board of directors made up of some recognizable names—men who thought they were part of a cutting-edge venture.

But here is what was really happening: he was a modern-day Peter Panhandler, taking money from wealthy women he charmed, then using it to keep his lavish life afloat and his business illusion alive.

Those private jets were paid for by someone else.
Those lavish dinners were funded by another woman's "investment."
The business was a shell game.

He was juggling money, keeping just enough spinning to make it look real. Eventually, the walls caved in.

The Fall of Maxwell

A lawsuit surfaced, filed by one of the women he conned. It dragged in the board of directors—men who thought they were in on the ground floor of a legitimate empire.

When the truth started unraveling, so did Maxwell. He packed a bag and fled to Mexico. He ended his life there.

That is how his story ended. There was no redemption arc, no apology, just the final act of a man who ran out of lies.

What I Should Have Noticed

When a man feels overly polished, trust that the performance has been practiced.

If he talks more about investors than intimacy, believe him. That is what he is really after.

A man who rushes from romance into business is not falling in love. He is scouting his next business source.

Lavish lifestyles with no visible income are not success. That is a scam in designer clothing.

Takeaway

A man who over-promises opportunities is usually under-delivering reality.

If he can pivot from "I want you" to "I want your money" in the time it takes to finish dessert, **RUN**.

When someone dazzles you with wealth and connections, ask who is really footing the bill.

If you are asked to loan him money, fund his projects, or "invest" in his ideas, stop immediately.

Someone who moves fast to merge finances is waving a massive red flag.

Lesson

The most convincing scam artists do not look like criminals; they look like charmers.

If a man moves lightning-fast from romance into "let me share my vision," it is not romance. It is recruitment.

The men who claim they are saving the world often cannot save themselves.

If the math does not add up, trust the numbers.

Love is not a loan. You are not his bank.

Red Flags to Remember

He always had "investors," but none of it was real. It was a revolving door funded by other people's money.

His charm was a weapon designed to pull both men and women into his schemes.

He disappeared the moment accountability arrived, leaving lawsuits and betrayal behind him.

Mic-Drop Truth

Some men wine and dine you. Others wine, dine, and redefine you into their next funding source.

Maxwell built an empire on smoke, mirrors, and other people's wallets.

In the end, even he could not afford his own lies, nor could he outlive them.

Brandy – The Liquor Liar

(aka: The Walking Hangover)

Brandy looked polished on the surface: suave, well-dressed, working for a big-name spirits company.

I met him thinking, *Oh, finally a man with some polish*. He was charming, funny, and always had a bottle of something rare and expensive to share. It all felt refined. He even organized a curated wine tote with special wines for one of my girlfriend weekends.

But here is the thing about men who work in booze: they are often just marinated in lies.

The Two-Woman Shuffle

Brandy was the classic double-life guy.

He had one story for me: "I cannot see you this weekend. I am spending time with my daughter."

Sounds noble, right? Except the truth was simpler and uglier. Months later, I discovered he was juggling two women at the same time—me in the Palm Desert area and another girlfriend in Orange County.

So, while he was telling me he was being a good dad, he was really just being a good liar. The truth always shows up eventually, whether you invite it or not.

The Thanksgiving Red Flag

The first crack came at Thanksgiving.

I invited him to my desert house while my parents were visiting. That was not casual. That was me opening a door and saying, *You matter.*

He showed up late, very late. When I finally asked why, he brushed it off with the same familiar excuse: "I was with my daughter."

I let it slide because of holiday traffic, family obligations, and the benefit of the doubt. Still, something lodged in my body. It was not panic nor was it anger. It was just a quiet note taken.

The Soirée Interrogation

A couple of months later, in January, I hosted a small soirée at my desert house. There were friends, dinner, laughter—the kind of night that shows you who someone really is when they walk into a room.

Brandy arrived late again. This time, hours late with the same excuse. "My daughter." This time, someone else noticed.

One of my girlfriends looked him straight in the eye and said, "Oh sure. You weren't late because of your daughter. You were late because you're seeing another woman."

The room went quiet.

Brandy snapped back immediately, defensive and sharp. "What are you talking about? That's not true." Then he turned to me. "You're going to let her talk to me like that?"

I did not rush to defend him. I did not scold her either. I simply said, "She sees something. She has the right to ask. You can answer."

He laughed it off, changed the subject, and slid right past it. Dinner continued, but the truth had already walked into the room. I just did not ask it to stay yet.

The Pattern Reveals Itself

Looking back, the timeline mattered.

He met me in the fall. Thanksgiving came and went with excuses. New Year's Eve? He canceled at the last minute. January brought the soirée and the confrontation.

By the winter months, nothing stacked up anymore. He was chronically late, chronically unavailable, and chronically defensive when questioned. Men who are honest do not live in a constant state of explanation.

I did not end things with a dramatic breakup speech. I simply stopped taking his calls. When someone keeps showing you exactly how little you matter, the most powerful response is silence.

What I Should Have Noticed

If he always smells like whiskey and secrets, believe the scent. A man who pours charm like top-shelf liquor usually waters down the truth.
"Spending time with my daughter" was just the mixer. His double life was the real cocktail.
If multiple people see the same red flag before you do, pay attention. Chronic lateness is not a timing issue. It is a priority issue.

Takeaway

A man who cannot show up on time will not show up when it matters. Your friends will clock his behavior long before your heart catches up. Listen. If a man works in spirits but kills yours, walk away.

Lesson

Anyone who constantly hides behind "family obligations" to explain their absence is usually hiding something or someone.

The smoothest talkers often have the slipperiest truths.

Red Flags to Remember

He was always late, always with an excuse.

He became defensive the moment someone questioned his story.

He expected me to manage the fallout from his lies in public.

When a man flips the script and makes you feel guilty for asking for respect, the red flag is already waving itself.

Mic-Drop Truth

Brandy did not just leave a bad taste in my mouth. He was the hangover I should have walked away from the second the bottle cracked.

Sometimes the smoothest pour is just a double shot of lies.

Johnny – The Outlaw

(aka: The Train Wreck Legacy)

Does the name Jesse James ring a bell?

This next one was literally a descendant of the infamous outlaw himself. Yes, his last name was James.

Here is the twisted part of this story. My own family had a brush with the original Jesse James. My great-grandmother's first husband, a wealthy and successful banker, was killed by Jesse James' gang during a train robbery in the late 1800s.

So, imagine the cosmic joke when, 130 years later, I ended up dating Jesse James' descendant.

The Charmer with a Dark Twist

Johnny was a businessman, decent-looking, and fun in that let's-go-have-a-cigar-and-drink-wine kind of way. He had that smooth, self-assured vibe that makes you think, *Well, maybe this one's different.*

We spent time together, went down to Mexico for the Fourth of July, hung out at cigar bars and classy restaurants. On the surface, it felt like an adventure, but underneath it all, Johnny was disconnected.

The Three-Month Rule Test

As always, I stuck to my three-month rule. I do not sleep with anyone until I have taken the time to really see who they are.

So, I waited. I thought, *Maybe after three months of getting to know him, dinners, beach walks, and good conversation, this could finally feel real. Eventually, I let that wall down.*

The very first night we were intimate, he literally rolled over afterward and said: "You can leave if you want to." He did not say it in the morning. He did not say it gently. He said it that night, like it had all been a transaction, neatly checked off his list.

The Mexico Meltdown

As if Mr. Bedside Manners was not enough, the final straw came during our trip to Mexico.

I took my Jeep across the border, paid for the insurance, and planned everything. Once we were there, he might as well have been traveling alone. He was far more interested in shooting fireworks on the beach than creating sparks with me.

When I finally called him out on his lack of attention, it turned into tears, fighting, and the usual emotional chaos.

On the way back, we smuggled cigars across the border. Johnny the Outlaw's idea, of course.

It was a mess from start to finish.

The Family Curse

Looking back, it felt like the universe was playing a dark joke.

Jesse James killed my great-grandmother's first love during a train robbery. Generations later, his descendant metaphorically robbed me of my time, patience, and emotional energy.

It was highway robbery and a complete train wreck, fitting for the family legacy.

What I Should Have Noticed

When a man brags about his outlaw bloodline, believe him. He will rob you in his own way.

If he treats your heart like a layover and intimacy like a pit stop, that is not romance. It is convenience.

A man who lights up more for cigars and fireworks than for you is already showing you where you rank.

The minute he rolled over and offered me the door, I should have realized I was never invited to stay.

Takeaway

A man who treats intimacy like a box to check will never give you real connection.

If his energy feels disconnected before the three-month mark, sleeping with him will not magically change that.

Someone who prioritizes his own thrill over your feelings will never make space for a real partnership.

Lesson

Johnny taught me that a man who acts interested just enough to keep you around, but never actually shows up emotionally, is not confused. He is simply not that into you.

No amount of waiting or hoping can manufacture connection where it does not exist.

Red Flags to Remember

He dismissed me emotionally the moment he got what he wanted.

When called out, he escalated instead of reflecting.

A man who makes you feel like you are on the sidelines of your own relationship is not worth your time.

Mic-Drop Truth

Johnny was not an outlaw. He was just emotionally MIA.
When the writing is on the wall, or in the family history, believe it.

SECTION III: The Gross-Out Files – When Red Flags Turn Cringe

Charm only goes so far. These were the men whose habits, lifestyles, and behaviors did not just raise concerns—they erased attraction entirely. What began as tolerance turned into discomfort, then outright revulsion, reminding me that when self-care, boundaries, and maturity are missing, everything else erodes with them. Ignoring non-negotiables does not make you open-minded. It makes you complicit in lowering your own standards and calling it growth.

Teaser: "These were not just red flags. They were full-body warning systems."

Trevor – The Tree Man
Grant – The Trophy Titan
Marvin – The Pus-Picking Human Ashtray
Tom – The Trailer Park Charmer

Trevor – The Tree Man

(aka: Paul Bunyan)

Trevor was from my rugged phase, very early in my life. You know the type. He's the guy who shows up smelling like sawdust, driving a beat-up truck overflowing with branches, leaves, and tools.

He owned a small landscaping business, which sounded kind of charming in theory. *Oh, he works with his hands. He's grounded, a real salt-of-the-earth guy.*

Yeah, he was grounded in dirt.

The Red Flag Truck

I should have known the first time he rolled up to take me out dancing. It was one of the few times he actually picked me up. His truck bed was literally full of half-dead tree limbs, freshly cut. We were about to go out for a fun night, and this man pulls up in what looked like a rolling compost heap. Branches were poking out everywhere, sawdust coated the seats, and he had not bothered to clean a thing.

And did I run? No.

I was young. I was dumb. I thought, *He's cute. Who cares if I am covered in mulch?*

Dancing with a Lumberjack

So, we went dancing. Honestly, he was fun in a chaotic, I-am-just-here-for-a-good-time kind of way.

After a couple of weeks, it became obvious. Trevor was not ambitious. He was not building some landscaping empire. He was cutting trees by day, drinking beer by night, and repeating the same cycle over and over.

He had no goals, no drive, just the same routine on loop.

Same Night, Same Bar

Trevor's life ran on repetition: the same bar, the same nights, the same beers, the same friends—week after week.

He lived from job to job and paycheck to paycheck, blowing whatever money he made on beer and cigarettes. There was no talk of what came next, no plans, no curiosity about anything beyond tonight.

We did not really "date." We mostly met up, always at the same country-western bar. He would pull straight into the parking lot after work, truck still full of branches and dust, ready to drink and dance like it was any other night. I went along with it because I liked dancing with him. The attention felt easy and, I was young and not asking myself the right questions yet.

Then one night it hit me. *What are we even doing here?*

There was no relationship forming and no momentum; there was only repetition. I was spending my time inside someone else's routine instead of building my own.

Not long after, I took a job and moved to Texas, far enough away to start fresh.

Trevor stayed exactly where he was.

What I Should Have Noticed

If a man cannot even clean his truck before picking you up, he is not thinking beyond bare-minimum effort.
"Rugged" is only cute until you realize it is just aimless.
A man who is stuck in the dirt is rarely looking to grow beyond it.

Takeaway

He might be handy with a chainsaw, but he is not exactly cutting down a path toward anything more.

Sometimes, the outdoorsy "Paul Bunyan" guy is not rugged and grounded. Sometimes, he is just stuck in the woods.

Lesson

Trevor taught me that a man without drive stays exactly where he is.

He had no growth, no goals, just the same routine on repeat. He was cutting trees by day, drinking beer by night, and never moving forward.

If you stay too long, you will find yourself stuck right there with him, breathing in cigarette smoke and sawdust in the passenger seat of his tree-limb-filled truck.

Red Flags to Remember

He was not building anything, just maintaining the same small circle.

His comfort zone was his cage, and he had no plans to leave it.

He did not lack potential. He lacked desire to do anything more.

Yes, hot guys can still smell like chainsaws and regret.

Mic-Drop Truth

A man without ambition will not build a future because he is perfectly fine staying right where he is.

Grant – The Trophy Titan

(aka: The Discount Ken Doll)

On paper, Grant looked like a catch. He had played professional tennis on the circuit and was still a titan at his country club. Charming, athletic, popular. He played golf, he was social, he had connections. Everyone at the club thought he was successful and put together.

Behind the scenes, he was a complete wreck.

The Human Ashtray Secret

Grant was a closet smoker.

At the club, no one knew. He kept that image pristine: fit, clean-cut, disciplined. But when it was just us, he would light up one cigarette after another, like a human ashtray.

The smoke was not the only thing he hid.

He also had a violent temper. He would go from calm to full-blown rage in seconds: yelling, screaming, and exploding without warning.

Like many men protecting fragile egos, he projected his insecurities outward and labeled me selfish the moment I challenged him.

The Wigging Out Birthday

For my birthday, we went to my favorite restaurant in Laguna Beach. I decided to do something playful, one of my favorite games called "Wigging Out," where you wear a wig and become a new character.

I arrived early wearing a brunette wig. At the time, I was blonde, so it was a full transformation. Grant walked in and looked around. The bartender and I were the only people in the bar. He looked directly at me, then away, then back again, clearly confused.

I stood up, smiling, and walked toward him. He looked panicked, like he was thinking, Who is this strange woman coming toward me?

"Hi," I said. "It is me."

He immediately snapped, irritated and not joking in the slightest. "What? What? You've got a wig on? You are so selfish. I am getting to know a blonde girl, and now you're a brunette? That is so selfish of you to wear a wig!"

He went on and on, scolding me for being playful.

So, I took the wig off, my hair a mess underneath, and sat through my birthday dinner completely deflated while he sulked about how "inconvenient" it was for him that I had a sense of humor.

My Dream Was Not About Him

Months later, the selfish accusation resurfaced.

I had been given an incredible opportunity to expand my business: opening a new office and working with clients across the entire state of California. It was my dream, the chance I had been working toward for years.

I shared the exciting news with him. He responded without hesitation. "You're selfish. You're leaving me. You're leaving us."

We had been dating maybe six months, and suddenly my career advancement, my hard-earned success, was framed as a personal betrayal.

That was it for me. When a man cannot celebrate your growth, or worse, makes you feel guilty for it, you know exactly where you stand.

The Dancing Insult

One night, while Grant was visiting me at my desert house, we went out dancing.

It was a lively place, full of music and energy. At one point, an older gentleman approached me while Grant stood right beside me and said, "Wow, you're a really good dancer. You're beautiful out there. Grant, you're a lucky man to have her."

A secure partner would have smiled and agreed. Grant did not. Instead, he looked at the man deadpan and said, "Great. Then take her. You can have her. Take her."

He showed no pride, no warmth, just a petty, snide little jab, because in that moment, someone else had noticed my light and he could not tolerate it.

The Therapy Project That Failed

Like so many women, I thought maybe I could help him heal.

When the volatility wore me down, I suggested therapy. I did not just suggest it, I paid for it. I sat beside him in the therapist's office, hoping someone else could reach the part of him I could not.

He nodded at the right times. He participated. He said the right things. Yet he walked out exactly the same man he had been when he walked in. Therapy could not fix him, because he did not want to be fixed.

The Tragic Ending

Years later, long after we were done, I learned that Grant had taken his own life.

It was heartbreaking. Beneath the temper, control, and image management was a pain he never learned how to soothe. It was tragic, and proof that no amount of love from the outside can repair a war raging on the inside.

I could not save him, and it was never my job to do. But I still remember that underneath all the smoke and ego was a deeply broken man.

What I Should Have Noticed

When a man calls your joy "selfish," he is revealing his insecurity, not your flaw. If he hides his own darkness and projects it onto you, it will not stop. It will escalate.

Takeaway

Sometimes the men who look like trophies are the most fragile of all. They may shine in public, but behind closed doors, they will slowly tarnish your joy if you let them.

Lesson

Playfulness and independence are only threats to insecure people.
You cannot fix someone who is committed to staying broken.
Men who call you selfish for being yourself will never truly support you.

Red Flags to Remember

He turned lighthearted moments into attacks.
Your success became a threat instead of a celebration.

He saw admiration from others as competition.

He needed you to manage his emotions, but never managed his own.

Mic-Drop Truth

Grant may have been a "trophy," but he belonged on a clearance rack: shiny, overvalued, and cheap to the touch.

Marvin – The Pus-Picking Human Ashtray

(aka: 'Starvin' Marvin)

Some men come with one red flag. Marvin arrived with a parade.

From the start, he was a smoker. He was not a casual smoker but a full-blown, ashtray-breath, nicotine-stained-fingers, hiding-it-but-not-really kind of smoker. I already knew smoking was a non-negotiable for me. It was one of those boundaries you draw before you even meet someone.

But dating has a way of testing your resolve. Sometimes you think, maybe I will let this one slide just this once. You should not, because Marvin did not just smoke. He picked.

The Pockmark Problem

Marvin was a grown man in his fifties who would sit across from me and absentmindedly squeeze the pockmarks on his face until pus came out. When he was done, he would wipe it on his jeans as if this was completely normal behavior.

Picture trying to have a conversation while watching someone casually extract fluids from their face—squish, wipe, then continue talking like nothing happened.

My stomach turned more times than I could count.

How I didn't leave the first time I saw it is still a mystery to me.

The Big Island Budget "Romance"

The real wake-up call came on our trip to the Big Island of Hawaii.

When we planned it, Marvin made big promises. He told me not to worry about food or excursions and said I would be spoiled. Based on that, we split the cost of the flight and hotel. It seemed fair.

It was not.

Once we arrived, everything changed. He paid for his own food and only his own food. He would grab his plate, eat, and then casually tell me I could get in line for mine.

Still, I did every time.

The excursions he promised suddenly became "too expensive." When we did go anywhere or do anything remotely fun, I paid my own way. That was when I realized I was not on vacation. I was on a budget lesson taught by a man who had no intention of being generous.

It was like dating Starvin' Marvin, a man cheap to the core, no matter the setting.

The Car Ride That Said It All

The tone for the entire trip was set before we even got on the plane.

Marvin owned a nice car. He lived in a house at a country club. On paper, he looked put together. However, when he came to pick me up for our Hawaiian vacation, he showed up in a car that looked like a rolling trash can.

Fast-food wrappers covered the seats and floorboard. Old coffee cups were crammed into the cupholders. Crumbs, trash, and random debris were everywhere. The smell was stale, a mix of smoke and old takeout.

I nearly gagged.

That was the moment I should have trusted my instincts. A man who cannot be bothered to clean the car he uses to pick you up for vacation is not a man who cares about details, comfort, or you.

The Essence You Cannot Escape

Even in paradise, you cannot escape someone's essence.

In Hawaii, Marvin still smoked. He still picked at his face. He still wiped whatever came out on his shorts without a second thought. Imagine sitting under a Hawaiian sunset, waves rolling in, palm trees swaying, while the man next to you casually squeezes his skin and flicks the residue away.

Paradise turned into purgatory quickly.

What I Should Have Noticed

When a man wipes pus on his pants mid-conversation, it is not just gross. He is telling you exactly who he is.
If his car looks and smells like a landfill, that is how he manages everything in his life.
A promise to "spoil you" that turns into "get in line and pay for your own food" is all the information you need.
Cheapness is not about money. It is about mindset.
If your body recoils before the trip even starts, listen to it.

Takeaway

No island, no sunset, and no romantic fantasy can disguise habits rooted in selfishness and neglect.
When your body reacts with disgust, it is not being dramatic. It is being honest.

You cannot polish an ashtray, and you sure as hell should not take one on vacation.

Lesson

Your non-negotiables exist for a reason. Do not talk yourself out of them.
A man who cannot invest in basic courtesy will never invest in you.
Cheapness is a character flaw, not a financial strategy.
How he treats his environment is how he treats relationships.

Red Flags to Remember

He treated basic hygiene as optional.
He smoked, picked, and wiped without regard for anyone else.
He brought the same stale energy everywhere, even to paradise.
He made bare-minimum effort into a lifestyle.

Mic-Drop Truth

You cannot kiss a man who smells like an ashtray and expect it to taste like romance.
Marvin was not just Starvin' Marvin. He was starving for self-respect, and I was done trying to feed it.

Tom – The Trailer Park Charmer

(aka: Casanova Cowboy of the Neon Lights)

Tom proudly gave himself the moniker Tin Can Tom because he lived in a trailer park. He said it like a badge of honor.

On our very first date, he told me—laughing—that his long-term ex of twenty years was living one street behind him in his fifth wheel. There was no marriage, no real commitment, just decades of proximity and familiarity.

He laughed again when he told me he had joked to the trailer park office that maybe he would move another girlfriend in too.

The woman shut it down immediately. "We don't want any of that around here."

Tom thought that part was funny. I should have realized then: this was not humor at all. It was normalization.

The Venus Flytrap Era

In his earlier dating days, Tom did not chase women. He waited.

He told me how he used to plant himself in familiar bars, familiar corners, familiar rooms, letting women drift into his orbit. Once a woman entered, he clamped down with charm and just enough attention to keep her circling.

He called it his Venus Flytrap era. I call it emotional ambush. He thought it was funny. I should have recognized it as a warning sign.

The Country-Western Loop

Years later, the setting changed, but the pattern did not.

He learned to country-western dance late in life. He lost a lot of weight, picked up a few dance moves, and suddenly the hits came faster: compliments, smiles, touch, and validation on demand.

He thrived on the praise we would get as we exited the dance floor. He loved being elevated to a better dancer than he actually was and was happy to collect the compliments while I quietly corrected his missteps under the neon lights.

I had been dancing my whole life. He had only just begun. What looked like chemistry was really just reflected shine.

The Addiction to Orbit

Tom was not really dating. He was feeding on attention.

The women orbiting him were not options; they were hits, and the dance floor became his dealer. It was a quick boost of attention to keep the emptiness quiet. He needed them the way some people need nicotine, sugar, or caffeine. That is why he went dancing almost every single night, with me or without me. That is where he got his fix.

Without orbiters, the silence would have been deafening.

The Charmer & the Ick

The ick did not arrive dramatically. It seeped in. At first it felt charming, then confusing, and eventually quietly repulsive.

Attraction does not die because of one gross moment. It dies when respect does not keep pace.

The Habits That Told on Him

Not everything was outright gross, but a lot of it was revealing.

He casually picked his nose while driving, the behavior of a man deeply committed to his own comfort, without a flicker of self-awareness.

Eeew. It was repulsive.

The rest lived on a spectrum.

He refused to use napkins, opting instead for self-folded paper towels kept everywhere, like security blankets. Not one or two, but stacks of them in his pockets, around his trailer, and eventually in my space, coffee-stained, food-stained, and always within reach.

Then there were the Circle K cups once full of cheap coffee and heavy creamer. These same disposable cups were endlessly reused and fiercely defended.

This was not about cleanliness. It was about rigidity, routines so locked in that there was no room for adjustment, curiosity, or another person's comfort.

These were not quirks. They were patterns, and patterns do not stay small. They revealed a man loyal to comfort, stalled in habit, and quietly resistant to change.

Blurred Lines

Tom told me he chose me. "I choose you. I've got your back." Yet the lines to other women never closed. He maintained no boundaries, no pause, and therefore no loyalty.

When I told him I could not stay in a relationship with open, emotionally entangled side doors, he did not misunderstand. He understood and chose not to change. That is not confusion. It is a choice.

The Dance That Ends

Tom did not know how to stay connected on the dance floor or in everyday life. He only knew how to move on or mentally check out. He would spin you, smile, and make you feel special, just long enough to keep moving.

Even while we were in a committed, exclusive relationship, his attention never fully stayed with me. His eyes scanned the room, clocking who was watching, acknowledging women he barely knew like they were someone special, sometimes behind my back, sometimes right in front of me.

He was not dancing with them. He was feeding on the attention they gave him. He mistook their attention for self-worth, and he performed intimacy instead of practicing it. He did not want a partner. He wanted a crowd.

It was fun in the moment but fleeting, with no roots, no real investment, just surface-level charm with no emotional depth behind it.

I left because he was disloyal and becoming increasingly disgusting. Once respect is gone, even the charm turns sour.

What I Should Have Noticed

He defended comfort at all costs. He replaced boundaries with orbiters and used validation as fuel. His words never matched his behavior.
If a man is constantly in motion, dancing with or entertaining everyone, do not expect him to slow down and stand still for you. He only stops when he is asleep.

Takeaway

Cringe is not chemistry. It is your instincts asking you to pay attention.
A man who blurs lines with other women and cannot respect your space will never respect your soul.

Lesson

When someone knows their behavior hurts you and continues anyway, they have already made their choice.

Red Flags to Remember

He was addicted to attention and performed intimacy instead of practicing it. He blurred lines with other women and never fully honored the relationship we shared.

And yes, he picked his nose. Enough said.

Mic-Drop Truth

He did not want a life partner. He wanted a dance partner, someone to move with him, make him look good under the lights, and check out when the music stopped.

He said he wanted commitment. What he actually wanted was commitment to the moment.

When I walked away, he proved it by contacting a friend of mine behind my back and asking her not to tell me. Loyalty was never part of the equation.

SECTION IV: Luxury, Lies & Illusions – When Money Masks the Truth

Not all heartbreak comes from men with nothing. Some came wrapped in luxury, jets, golf courses, and fine wine, while hiding selfishness, deception, or a wife in the background. They dazzled me with illusion, but when the shine faded, the truth was darker than I imagined.

Teaser: "Even red flags look chic on a private jet."

Sterling – The Married Millionaire
Preston – The Trust Funder
Vinny – The Mobster in Disguise

Sterling – The Married Millionaire

(aka: Mr. Jet-Set Secrets)

Just like his name, everything about him glittered like it had been dipped in gold.

When I first met him, he told me directly that he was separated and preparing for divorce. With Sterling, it was easy to believe. He was polished, charming, and effortless. He noticed the shoes I was wearing immediately. They were Donald Pliners. He knew the brand, the cut, the style without hesitation.

That is the kind of man Sterling was: impeccable taste, a keen eye for detail, and a way of making you feel like the most exquisite person in the room. He would take me to upscale restaurants for dinner and dancing, yet he was equally comfortable country-western dancing in a dusty dive bar in the middle of nowhere.

He moved easily between luxury and laid-back charm.

Greens, Jets & Chrome

Sterling's life revolved around golf courses. He owned six homes that stretched from the desert oasis of California to the mountains of Utah and Montana. Each one was perched perfectly on manicured greens, as if the fairways were extensions of his private kingdom.

Evenings with him felt magical and unpredictable. We would hop on his golf cart and cruise around PGA West after the sun dipped low, driving straight through the sprinklers and laughing like children. Sometimes we would sneak over to the golf ponds at night and pretend to fish simply for the thrill of doing something we were not supposed to do.

Of course, Sterling was an incredible golfer. He liked to turn the game into playful challenges. He would say, "If I make this impossible shot, I owe you a new pair of Jimmy Choos." He always made the shot. He would then walk into the boutique and purchase the thousand-dollar shoes without hesitation.

Golf was only part of his world.

Sterling owned two private jets. They were not chartered. They were his. He was a licensed pilot, and I often sat beside him in the cockpit as he lifted us off the runway and into another spontaneous weekend. We might begin in the desert and land a few hours later in Montana or Utah, headed toward another home, another sunset, and another carefully planned adventure.

His garage resembled a cross between a luxury showroom and a racetrack. It housed a dozen high-end cars, two race cars, and several collector motorcycles, including multiple Harleys. He employed a full-time mechanic whose sole responsibility was maintaining his vehicles.

Sometimes we would take a Harley out at sunset, the desert air warm against my face. Other times we selected a different car depending on the mood, choosing a sports car for speed, a luxury sedan for elegance, or a race car when he was headed to the track.

Time with Sterling was not merely exciting. It was meticulously engineered to be unforgettable.

The Soul Connection

The glamour was only part of it. With Sterling, there was an aching emotional connection I had never experienced before.

We would sit together in silence with our eyes locked and feel a deep longing that went beyond words. Sometimes we would cry together. It stirred something profound within me and led me back to writing poetry and painting.

One morning he asked softly, "Have we met before? I feel as though I have known you in another life." In that moment, I believed him.

Life Like a Cocktail

Life with Sterling was like the perfect cocktail, smooth and intoxicating, strong enough to leave you dizzy with delight.

He also possessed a sly humor that revealed just how self-aware he could be. He once said, "I take my friends out for cocktails, and then I have to sit there and listen to the cocktails talk back to me."

That was Sterling in essence. He created the indulgence and later mocked it with a wry grin.

The Truth Comes Out

For months, I believed his story that he was separated, soon-to-be divorced, and free to love again. One afternoon, whether by chance or by the universe exposing his dirty little secret, I spotted him at PGA West, cruising in his golf cart with a stunning woman seated beside him.

In that moment, I knew. She was not "someone he was casually seeing" or "a lingering ex." She was his wife. The lie hit me like a golf ball straight to the gut. I did not need any explanations, excuses, or another round of elaborate storytelling served up with cocktails.

I ended the relationship immediately and did not look back.

Years Later

Years after the breakup, I was at a bar with a friend when Sterling suddenly appeared. I did not see him approaching. He walked straight up to me, kissed me boldly on the lips as if no time had passed, and left me breathless.

My friend, who had never met him, stared and said, "Oh, that must be Sterling."
Of course, it was.

What I Should Have Noticed

When a man claims he is "separated" yet there are women's clothes in the closet and a flat iron on the counter, he is not separated. He is stalling.
I should have questioned the line, "She just stays here for girls' weekends." Uh-huh, and I am just here for the décor.
I should have paid more attention to how seamless everything felt, how rehearsed the charm was, and how every moment sparkled a little too perfectly. Even during our quiet, emotional moments, something inside me hesitated. Deep down, I understood that men this polished often conceal a mess behind the curtain.
He was not simply teeing up romance. He was running a parallel life. I ignored my intuition because the glitter was so damn convincing.

Takeaway

Wealth does not equal integrity. Luxury can mask the ugliest lies.
A man who claims he is "separated" while still sharing a home with his wife is not separated.
If his story does not make sense the first time, it will not make sense the tenth.

Lesson

Sterling taught me that even the most polished lifestyle can contain cracks large enough to fall through.
A man who keeps one foot planted in his former life will never fully step into yours.

Red Flags to Remember

Women's clothing in the closet of a man who insists he is separated and divorcing.

An explanation that she only uses the house for "girlfriend weekends" is not reasonable.

A persistent twinge in your gut that you keep talking yourself out of believing.

Mic-Drop Truth

A man can flash a black Amex and still be bankrupt where it matters most: integrity, loyalty, and truth.

Even the most dazzling man, the one who plays the perfect game, makes every shot, and promises you the world, can still be living in the rough.

Preston – The Trust Funder

(aka: The Fountain Fob Fool)

On paper, Preston looked like the kind of man who had it all: a hillside home overlooking the harbor, a family name that opened doors, and a lifestyle that sounded effortless.

In reality, he was the kind of man who never really worked a day in his life.

He lived off the safety net of his wealthy father's company, carried just enough responsibility to make it seem like he had a "career," and filled the rest of his days with long lunches, surfing, and tennis matches.

The Resume of Red Flags

Preston had already been married once to an heiress from a prominent island family whose fortune came from building a massive transportation system generations ago. They had two kids together, but when the marriage ended, he didn't fight for them.

Instead, he made a deal: she kept the kids, and he walked away with a huge financial settlement.

That should have been the only red flag I needed because a man who can trade his kids for a paycheck is telling you exactly who he is. But I ignored it, thinking, *Maybe he just didn't want a messy custody battle.*

Let me save you some time. Never ignore that one.

The Dog Who Knew Better

Preston even had a dog that was a sweet, loyal thing who only wanted to be walked and loved. But Preston rarely bothered.

When I came around, the dog's tail would explode with excitement because finally it meant he would get to go outside, sniff the harbor breeze, and have some freedom. We would walk him all the time along the Dana Point Harbor. I could almost feel the dog thanking me with every wag.

It hit me one day: even this dog was neglected by a man who could not care about anything beyond his own comfort.

The Illusion of Generosity

In the beginning, Preston seemed generous. He took me out, told colorful stories about his past, and even brought me a beautiful piece of jewelry after one of his worldly trips. It was an exotic black pearl necklace from his trip to a faraway island, gorgeous and presented like a gesture of romance.

But like everything with Preston, the generosity was just for show.

The Car That Did Not Make the Cut

There was one moment that should have told me everything. Preston explained, calmly and without shame, that my car did not really fit the neighborhood. He suggested that instead of parking it on the street, I should pull it into his driveway and hide it behind his other cars. He presented it as helpful and practical, as if he was doing me a favor.

What struck me later was the irony. I had worked for everything I owned and took care of what I had. It was not flashy, but it was clean, well-maintained, and fully mine.

What bothered him was not responsibility or quality. It was image. In that moment, I realized I was being asked to shrink, not because I did not belong there, but because I did not fit the picture he wanted to present.

The Crybaby Moment

One night, he threw a catered party at his house. I invited a few friends, thinking it would be a nice evening. Wine, music, good food, you know, the kind of night where you think, *Okay, maybe this man really is worth my time.*

And then, after everyone left, he turned to me and said, "Since they were your friends, you should split the cost of the party with me."

Excuse me?

This was a man who literally never worked for a dime of his wealth, standing in his luxury home, arguing with me over splitting a small catering bill. When I refused, he did what spoiled men do when they do not get their way: he threw a tantrum.

He grabbed what he thought were my car fob and keys, stormed out to the driveway, and hurled them straight into the fountain in front of his house.

Except they were not mine. They were his. His key fob sank into his own fountain, hundreds of dollars disappearing beneath the surface along with whatever pride he thought he had left.

The Exit

I calmly picked up my fob and keys, which he hadn't managed to grab, and left without saying a word. I was just done.

I drove away while he stood in his driveway, staring at his own fob at the bottom of his fountain, realizing he had just screwed himself.

What I Should Have Noticed

A man who prioritizes his bank account over his own kids will always prioritize it over you.

A dog that only lights up when you walk in? That is a living clue about the neglect he dishes out.

If he throws a tantrum over a bill, don't walk. **RUN**.

Takeaway

A trust fund does not guarantee a full heart. A man with money can still be emotionally bankrupt.

Lesson

Preston taught me that wealth without humility is just entitlement. Access to money does not mean access to character or the capacity to truly care.

Even his own dog knew the truth. He did not care—not about the dog, not about his kids, not about me, not about anyone.

Red Flags to Remember

Flaunting a trust fund like it is a personality trait.

Expecting the world to cater to him without lifting a finger.

Confusing privilege with worth, and control with generosity.

Mic-Drop Truth

A man who thinks his bank account is his identity will never invest in anything real.

He may have been born with a silver spoon, but he could not carry the weight of a real relationship.

Vinny – The Mobster in Disguise

(aka: Mr. Phony Baloney)

The Funny Guy with a Golf Swing

We met online, and a few conversations in, I was hooked. He was funny, confident, and charming in that effortless entertainer way. He played golf, cracked jokes constantly, and made me laugh so much I thought, *Wow, this guy is actually refreshing.*

So, we met for lunch. He was cute, relaxed, and easy to talk to. For a while, it felt like I had finally found someone who was as funny and lighthearted as he was engaging.

But Vinny had layers.

The Mobster Legacy Reveal

Over time, he dropped the mobster family bombshell. One day, he casually handed me two books, both written about his family. Turns out, his grandfather and great-uncles were big-time mob bosses in Chicago back in the day.

I thought, *Is this guy serious? Am I about to be in a real-life Sopranos episode?* I will not lie, part of it was intriguing. Who would not be curious about someone tied to a family legacy like that?

He carried himself like a man who knew people. He gave off that mobster-lite vibe, part "don't worry, I got this" and part "you better not cross me."

Here is the thing. Underneath that polished, mobster charm, Vinny was a mess.

The Health Bombshell He Hid

At first, we would go out, laugh, drink, eat sushi, and have a good time. He did not let on that anything was wrong. He ate red meat, drank booze, and acted like he was bulletproof.

Then one day, he got sick, really sick. He called me from bed saying he did not feel well, so I asked what was going on. That is when he dropped it: "Oh, by the way, I had half my intestines removed. Colon cancer."

"I'm sorry. You had what?"

This was not a small detail. It was major, and he had completely hidden it. He was literally risking his health every day while pretending everything was fine.

Sedona, the Awkward Kiss & the Daughter Drama

At one point, he planned this big romantic trip to Sedona. I thought, *Maybe it would bring us closer.*

It did not.

We went on a beautiful picnic, the perfect desert backdrop, and he lunged in for this big, dramatic kiss that landed so wrong it made me cringe. He completely misread my body language. The timing was not right, and it was just awkward.

During the remainder of the trip, he would not stop whining about one of his daughters who hated him. It was on loop. Every single moment was about how she did not like him.

What was supposed to be romantic turned into a therapy session I never signed up for.

The Final Straw

The end came when he got sick again. I went over to help, brought the things he asked for, showed up when he needed me. But then I found out another woman had already been there taking care of him. He had not told me she existed, just like he had not told me the full truth about his health.

That was it. I was done.

What I Should Have Noticed

A man who hides major health issues is capable of hiding anything.
Constant whining about "who wronged him" is a sign he is living in victim mode.
Family drama is a preview of the emotional weight you will end up carrying.

Takeaway

A man with mobster charm might seem fun, but if he is careless with his health and hides major truths, he will be careless with you too.

Lesson

Vinny taught me that charm can distract you from the cracks in someone's foundation, but eventually, those cracks show.

Red Flags to Remember

Handing you books about his mob family is not romantic; it is foreshadowing.
Eating like nothing is wrong while hiding that half his intestines are gone is more than reckless; it is deceitful.
If he makes you his therapist about his "woe is me," you are not a partner, you are a crutch.

Mic-Drop Truth

If he cannot take care of himself or be honest about it, he will never take care of you.

Section V: Users & Freeloaders – The Cost of Carrying a Grown Man

These are the men who coast. The ones who take advantage and contribute nothing, whether in your home or to your giving nature. They charm their way into your life and quietly begin feeding off your generosity, hospitality, time, or emotional support without ever reciprocating. They believe their mere presence is contribution enough. At first, it feels like kindness, but eventually it feels like being used. It is not what they take in a day, but rather what they take over time.

Teaser: "These guys did not just bring baggage. They moved into mine."

Randy – The Golfing Couch Surfer
Howard – The Therapy Sponge
Ethan – The Contractor Who Never Showed Up

Randy – The Golfing Couch Surfer

(aka: The Couch Caddie)

Meet Randy. He was the kind of man who could light up a room the second he walked in, handsome and athletic, with an effortless charm that made you think, *Maybe this one has potential.*

Spoiler: he did not.

The Trauma That Froze Him

When Randy was six years old, his father was killed by a drunk driver. That single moment shaped him forever. He never touched a drop of alcohol; it was his quiet rebellion against fate.

While he stayed clean on the outside, the inside was stuck. Randy lived like someone who pressed pause on his life decades ago and never figured out how to hit play again.

The Wellness Hustle That Was Not His

When I met him, he was "half owner" of a wellness company selling infrared saunas and healthy living products. On the surface, it sounded impressive.

Except the truth was this: Betty, his current roommate and business partner, actually owned the company. She gave him half of it out of affection, and perhaps because she never stopped holding a torch for him.

Betty handled the books, ran the finances, and even covered more of the shared household expenses, especially since her daughter also lived there. They were not romantically involved, at least not on his side. Randy was very clear he did not want that, but Betty never fully let go.

When she found out I was done dating him after nearly three years of whatever we were, she tried to move back in emotionally and said, "We're supposed to be together."

He told her no, but with Randy, nothing was ever fully severed. He would not bite the hand that fed him. If someone was willing to cover the bills and carry the weight, he stayed.

The Story I Should Have Heard

Early on, Randy told me a story about a man he knew who fell in love with a wealthy woman and ended up living comfortably off her success. He told it like it was romantic. He even added that if something like that ever happened to him, it would be a great story.

I remember nodding and letting it pass. At that time, it did not register as a warning. It sounded harmless, almost hypothetical.

Looking back, it was not hypothetical at all. It was his philosophy.

Randy did not see financial dependence as temporary or embarrassing. He saw it as acceptable, comfortable, and even ideal.

When someone tells you the kind of life they would happily live, believe them.

Dating Randy Was Like Dating a Pipe Dream

After six months, I knew he was not it, but somehow, I stayed.

We eventually shifted into a strange, semi-platonic arrangement with a side of couch surfing. He would stay at my place in the spare room, take care of my cats, clean the house, and be helpful in the day-to-day.

He was helpful, but never my equal.

He lived on potential that never materialized, talking big about how "I've got this idea that's really going to take off," and nothing ever did. He would start things, stall out, drift, and then talk himself into a new fantasy.

The Man Who Could Not Keep His Mouth Shut

Another thing about Randy? He could not keep his mouth shut about me. It was as if he had no story of his own, so he simply borrowed mine. To anyone who would listen—neighbors, golf buddies, the lady at the grocery store—he would brag about my business, my homes, the trips I had taken, and the things I had accomplished.

It was not malicious; it was needy.

I value my privacy. I like keeping a low profile. So, when I told him, more than once, "Randy, please stop talking about my life to people. Tell your story, not mine," you know what he did?

Naturally, he kept right on flapping his jaw.

One time, I had a brand-new neighbor move in next door. I had not even had a chance to introduce myself yet, and there was Randy out front giving them my entire resume.

It was infuriating, but also, so very Randy. There were no boundaries and no filter, just a man trying to matter in the only way he knew how.

Athletic But Aimless

Here is the kicker. On the golf course, Randy was phenomenal. He could play like a pro, shoot a par, even a hole-in-one. Yet in life, he never lived up to par. Honestly, I was not feeling randy about being randy with Randy anymore. That was the moment I knew it was time to let him and his endless promises of someday go.

The One Surprising Thing About Randy

For all his lack of direction, Randy did have one unexpected strength: his intuition. He could read other people and situations with uncanny accuracy and often sensed what was coming before it was spoken. There were moments when he seemed deeply tuned in, calm, perceptive, and surprisingly clear.

At times, his insight even supported my own work and creative process. It was one of the few areas where he appeared grounded and present. But like everything else with Randy, that awareness never translated into momentum. Insight without action became just another unrealized gift, another spark that never turned into a flame.

The Comfort That Kept Me Stuck

Randy was one of the men I stayed connected to the longest. We dated for nearly three years, and even after the romantic part ended, he did not really leave my life.

He stayed in my life, not as a boyfriend, but not as someone who was truly gone either. He couch-surfed at my place, helped with my cats when I traveled, and was woven into my day-to-day life. We talked constantly, shared ideas, laughed a lot, and in many ways, he became my closest companion.

That familiarity made it harder to see what was actually happening. There was no forward motion because I was not dating anyone else or opening space for something new. I already had someone there, filling the role of emotional company without the responsibility of partnership.

I told myself it was harmless because the romance was gone, but energy does not care about labels. An ex who still occupies emotional space is still in the way. As long as he was there, I was not fully available for anything else.

I was the one who ended it, not out of anger or resentment, but out of clarity. I told him I needed to stop talking, not because he was a bad person, but because the connection had become a comfortable pause instead of a path forward.

Letting go was not dramatic, and it was not difficult once I was honest with myself. It was necessary.

What I Should Have Noticed

Pipe dreams without action are just talk.
Someone can be helpful and sweet but still not your equal.
If he cannot respect your privacy or your boundaries, he will never create his own.
A man who is "comfortable" just existing will never suddenly wake up and start thriving.

Takeaway

A man who can hit the perfect shot on the course but cannot make a single move in life will always leave you waiting on potential that never comes, no matter how charming, spiritually gifted, or jaw-flappingly proud of you he might be.

Lesson

He was more committed to his golf swing than to any actual plans for the future.
His charm masked a lack of ambition and follow-through.
He talked a big game but lived like a perpetual guest in his own life.
If you want a new relationship, you have to make room for it. That means clearing space for something real, even when what you are letting go of feels familiar and safe.

Red Flags to Remember

A man who lives off other people's stability will always leave you footing the emotional bill.
Do not confuse temporary charm for long-term reliability.
If he is always "working on big plans" but never delivers, you are dealing with a dreamer, not a doer.

Mic-Drop Truth

He could shoot par on the golf course, but could not live up to par in real life.

Howard – The Therapy Sponge

(aka: Mr. Emotional Leech)

Meet Howard. On paper, he seemed sweet and sensitive, a guy "in touch with his emotions." He was the kind of man who talked about self-growth, read every self-help book ever written, and swore he was working on himself.

But the reality? Howard was not working on himself; he was just wallowing in himself.

Heavy Baggage Always Unpacked on Me

Howard had a tragic backstory, and trust me, I heard it on repeat. When he was young, his father committed suicide. Howard was the one who found him. It wrecked him. His whole life had been a trauma response from that moment forward.

His family dynamics were, to put it mildly, too close for comfort. He and his sister were practically inseparable, doing things together like a pseudo-couple. It was strange.

Instead of healing from it all, Howard just stayed stuck, talking endlessly about his trauma but never moving through it.

The Man Who Literally Could Not Sweat

This was the kicker. Howard literally could not sweat. When I met him, he was already on a years-long quest to figure out why his body refused to release toxins. He went to specialist after specialist without finding any answers. Somehow, it made perfect sense. He could not let anything go. He held it all in.

Years later, long after we had broken up, I heard he even wrote a self-help book about not sweating. Apparently, he learned how to sweat again and turned it into his "journey of transformation." Of course, he did.

Therapy, But Only for Him

I should have known better, but at the time I still believed I could "help."

I even took Howard to leftover therapy sessions I had originally purchased for another disaster (Grant, the Trophy Titan). I figured, *Hey, maybe this will help him process his stuff.*

It was a big mistake.

Howard sat on that therapist's couch and turned it into a Howard pity party. He cried, whined, and rehashed every detail of his trauma. The therapist glanced at me with that "oh honey, run" kind of look.

I realized I was not his girlfriend. I was his emotional sponge.

The Final Straw

One night, after yet another hours-long conversation about his feelings, I realized he had not asked me one single thing about mine. Not once. Howard wanted someone to hold space for his pain, but he had none left for anyone else.

I stopped being his sponge.

Here is the Funny Prequel

When we first crossed paths on the airport shuttle, I did not actually meet the real Howard. I met Howard wearing a toupee. I did not know it at the time, of course. He gave me his number and said, "Reach out if you're ever available."

Fast forward over a year later, after I finally ended things with another disaster, I called him. Before we even made plans, he confessed, "Karen, I have to tell you, when you met me, I was wearing a toupee. I don't wear it anymore."

The man I thought I had met was not even the real man, just a projection with fake hair. The fact that he finally ditched it? Just like his inability to sweat, it was a metaphor for him holding onto an image for far too long before finally dropping the act.

What I Should Have Noticed

When someone's entire identity is built around trauma, they will drain you dry.
If a man literally cannot sweat, he cannot release anything.
A man who only talks about feelings but never acts on change is not evolved; he is stuck.

Takeaway

A man who cannot release his past (or his toxins) will leave you holding it all.
You are supposed to be his partner, not his therapist, his detox plan, or the one peeling off his fake layers, hairpiece included.
Emotional dumping is not emotional depth.
If you feel more like a therapist than a partner, it is time to leave.

Lesson

Howard taught me that listening to someone's pain is not the same as building a life with them.
A man who only wants to process his trauma with you is not a partner; he is a project you never signed up for.

Red Flags to Remember

He lived in a constant state of self-pity without ever taking steps toward healing.

He left no room for your feelings because his always came first.
He confused trauma bonding with intimacy.

Mic-Drop Truth

A man who cannot sweat out his past will leave you drowning in it.
If he starts with a fake hairpiece, do not be surprised when the rest of the relationship is just as artificial.

Ethan – The Contractor Who Never Showed Up

(aka: The Jack Mormon)

The Meet-Cute on a Plane

Ethan was the rugged, tall outdoorsman I met on a plane while flipping through a mountain biking magazine. He sat down next to me, started chatting, and before we even landed, he asked, "Would you like to go out sometime?"

He lived in Northern California, and I was in Portland, Oregon, but we made it work at first. He would fly up to see me, and sometimes I would fly down to see him.

Ethan was handsome, kind, charming, a contractor, and a dad. The kind of man who looked like he could build a cabin with his bare hands. He seemed adventurous, like someone building something meaningful.

The truth was simpler. Ethan was an escape artist.

The Office I Ran While He Played Outside

Ethan moved me to Southern California so we could be together and help him run his new telecommunications business with his partner. I agreed, thinking it would be a true partnership, both in love and in business.

However, once I was there, it became clear who was actually running the business. I was the one managing the office, the schedules, the daily grind, while Ethan was off mountain biking, skiing, and spending time up north with his pack of kids.

When his business partner would ask, "Where's Ethan?" I would just smile and say, "That's between you and Ethan."

In reality, he was on a trail somewhere, avoiding adulthood.

The Jack Mormon Moment

Ethan was a Mormon, but not a fully practicing one. One day after skiing, we went down to the bar, and he ordered a shot of Jägermeister. I raised an eyebrow. "Isn't that liquor?" I asked. He shrugged and said, "That does not count. It is just Jägermeister." I laughed and told him, "That's called a Jack Mormon."

He blinked as if he never even heard the term before. I knew exactly what it meant, but he did not realize he was living the definition—picking the parts of his faith and his life that suited him and ignoring the rest.

The Final Flat Tire

At first, I tried to go along with the mountain biking and skiing adventures. I went several times, but most of the time, Ethan just went alone, disappearing into the trails while I held down the fort. He spent more time up north with his kids, his bike, and skis than down south, where I was left running everything else.

Eventually, I realized I was not in a partnership. I was a pit stop.

I was building stability while he chased adrenaline, and just like one of his flat tires, our relationship went flat. He never bothered to fix it.

What I Should Have Noticed

When you are running his office, his schedule, and his life while he is "finding himself" on a mountain, it is not balance; it is avoidance.

If he cannot commit to his own path, he cannot commit to yours.

A man who escapes into hobbies is escaping more than just stress. He is avoiding responsibility.

Takeaway

A man who prioritizes bike and ski trails over building a future will eventually leave you stranded.

Rugged looks can hide rugged priorities.

Lesson

A man who avoids his own life will always avoid showing up for yours.

Ethan taught me that being "handsome and kind" is not enough.

Red Flags to Remember

He had a business but barely showed up for it.

His religion became a convenient excuse.

His true love was not you or the work; it was the trail.

Mic-Drop Truth

If he cannot build his own foundation, he sure as hell cannot help you build yours.

Section VI: The Emotionally Misaligned – The Ones Who Could Not Meet Me Where I Was

Not every man was awful. Some were kind. Some were decent, but still wrong for me—too rigid, too stuck, too insecure, or too spiritually self-important. They reminded me what I did not want and clarified what I do deserve.

These were not sweeping disasters or elaborate con artists. They were simply men who were misaligned in ways that mattered. Some deflected their insecurities onto me the second they felt exposed. Some tried to mold me into their belief system as if I were a project. Some could not hold the same emotional depth or accountability I required. The gap was not always dramatic, but it was undeniable once I stopped pretending it was not there.

Compatibility is not just about shared interests or chemistry. It is about capacity. It is about whether two people are growing in the same direction at the same pace. These men were not villains, but they were not aligned either. They were teachers in discernment, revealing where I was settling, where I was overcompensating, and where I had outgrown the room.

Teaser: "Good men are not always the right men."

Peter – The Puny Pencil Pinky Pecker
Gideon – The Born-Again Zealot
Norman – When Mr. Normal Isn't Enough
Everett – The Trial Esquire

Peter – The Puny Pencil Pinky Pecker

(aka: Mr. Micro-Moment of Regret)

On the beach where I met him, he looked perfect. He was tall, broad-shouldered, six-foot-four, with a disarming smile and a charming little boy who made him seem even more lovable.

He was a lawyer, well-spoken, and confident. He was one of those men who gives off "I've got my life handled" energy. As expected, I followed my three-month rule. No intimacy until I really get to know you.

For three months, everything checked out. He was fun, attentive, and gave me just the right amount of flirty banter. I thought, *Okay, this might actually be something.*

The Almost Relationship

For three months, everything stayed comfortably on the surface. We spent most of our time at the beach enjoying long walks and easy conversation. It felt romantic in a simple, low-effort way.

He talked mostly about his work, opinions, and experiences. Even stories about his past relationships somehow looped back to him. I listened more than I was seen.

He came over to my place for dinner. I cooked, he showed up, we talked, and he left. This was our routine. He did take me out a few times, but there was never any real initiative behind it and no sense of direction. There was no intentional building of something deeper.

At the time, I told myself it was simple. I was new to California and I enjoyed the attention. I was not asking the right questions yet.

What I did not see then was that comfort without investment is often just avoidance dressed up as ease. It feels pleasant until you realize nothing is actually growing.

The Big Reveal or Not

We were finally in bed. The lights were low. The tension had built.

And then, well…

Let us just say, when I reached down, it felt like a cut-off pencil. This is not an exaggeration. This was the smallest manhood I had ever encountered in my life—about the size of my pinky finger. I literally found myself thinking, *I could not feel a thing.*

Do you know what he said with zero irony?

"Wow, you're a pretty full woman. I am used to really skinny, scrawny girls." *Excuse me? Sir, I am not the problem here.*

That is when it clicked. This was not about size. It was about shame. Instead of being present, he deflected and made me wrong in order to protect himself. His ego only showed up once it was bruised. That is when he weaponized it.

When the Image Cracked

The night did not recover after that moment. Instead of staying present, he pulled away. The confidence faded and the connection disappeared. What mattered most to him was not intimacy. It was regaining control of the situation.

Rather than acknowledge the awkwardness or meet the moment honestly, he deflected. He redirected the discomfort onto me as if something about my body or expectations had caused the disconnect. That was when I felt it: the urge to soften, to reassure him, and to shrink myself to protect his ego.

However, I did not.

The night ended early, and he did not stay. Once he left, the confusion lifted almost immediately.

This was not about compatibility. It was about a man who could maintain charm only as long as his image stayed intact. The moment it cracked, dismissal replaced connection.

What I Should Have Noticed

He steered conversations away from emotional depth and hid behind intellect.
His compliments carried a passive-aggressive edge.
He offered surface-level attention, but never truly saw me.

Takeaway

Confidence is not about bravado, job titles, or bedroom stats. It is about emotional presence, integrity, and the ability to hold space without shrinking from intimacy.

Lesson

When a man protects his ego by dismissing you instead of meeting the moment with honesty, the relationship is already unsafe.
The right response is not to shrink or reassure. It is to trust what your body and instincts are telling you and walk away.
Intimacy exposes what charm can hide.

Red Flags to Remember

He invests in persona and performance more than connection.
He talks about himself but rarely shows real curiosity about you.
He keeps dating easy and low-effort while avoiding depth.
When his confidence is challenged, he deflects and makes you the problem.
You feel the urge to make yourself smaller to protect his ego.

Mic-Drop Truth

If I feel myself shrinking to make a man feel bigger, I am already too small for the relationship I deserve. Besides that, he may have already come up short.

Gideon – The Born-Again Zealot in a Mercedes

(aka: The Mercedes Messiah)

Some men try to win you over with charm. Others try with success. Then there is the type who believes religion will do the trick.

Enter Gideon, the man who showed up in a shiny used Mercedes, like a kid playing dress-up in a suit two sizes too big. He looked put together at first, but the more layers you peeled back, the clearer it became that it was all decoration.

The First Impression

I met Gideon when he came into my home with his water restoration team to fix an upstairs leak. He was tall, friendly, athletic-looking, with just enough charisma to make me think, *Hey, this guy might be different.* He played golf and softball, and knew how to hold a conversation.

Here is the kicker. When the workday ended, Gideon did not drive off to his own home. He drove back to his mom's house, but not into the main house either. He lived in this little side room that had its own door, like a permanent guest who never outgrew his stay.

The Mercedes Mirage

He tried to mask it with the car. "I drive a Mercedes," he would say, smirking. Sure, that was technically true. It was a used Mercedes, bought just so he could look like he had money.

The reality was far less impressive. He was living with mom, saving pennies, and pretending he was one step from the good life.

The Religion Curveball

The real curveball came later.

Gideon was a born-again zealot, not just a casual Sunday-morning churchgoer. Oh no. He was the fire-and-brimstone type, the kind who would suddenly drop a "You need to come to church with me" over dinner like it was dessert.

I thought, *Okay, I'll give it a try. One service. One chance.*

The second I stepped into that place, I knew I could not do it. It was not about faith; it was about control. The way he looked at me after, as if I was supposed to feel guilty for not being as devoted as he was, made my skin crawl.

Faith is fine. Weaponized faith is a hard pass.

The Backstory

Then came the deeper truth. Gideon was a recovering meth addict.

Before I met him, he had spent years working in the construction industry before addiction derailed everything. By the time we were dating, he was clean. But the way he clung to religion made it clear it had simply replaced the chaos he never dealt with.

Underneath it all, he was still stuck.

The "Meet the Parents" Moment

For some reason, I let him meet my family: parents, brothers, the whole crew. After that, he actually looked me in the eye and said, "Well, I guess I've met everyone now." Like it was a checkbox, as if he thought that alone earned him a future with me.

Meanwhile all I could think was: You still live with your mom. You're recovering from meth. You're trying to convert me to a faith I don't believe in. And you think meeting my parents is going to seal this deal?

Not happening.

The Exit

When I finally ended it, there was not even a fight.

I just walked away. No explanation was needed. He was a nice enough man on the surface, but I knew if I stayed, I would end up in a tiny back room next to his mother's kitchen, being lectured about church while he pretended that a used Mercedes made him a success story.

That was a hard no.

What I Should Have Noticed

Living with his mom at that age is not "close family ties." It is emotional immaturity on full display.
Addiction does not disappear; it just finds a new outlet.
Anyone who tries to "save" you spiritually when you did not ask? **BYE.**

Takeaway

A shiny car cannot disguise a stalled life.
His "faith" was not about connection; it was about control dressed up as righteousness.
A man who is still trying to save himself cannot build a life with you.

Lesson

Faith, recovery, or even charm will not fix the fact that he is not truly ready to stand on his own.
Gideon taught me that a man still rebuilding himself cannot build a relationship with you.

Red Flags to Remember

He bragged about a used Mercedes like it erased the fact that he still lived with his mom.
His "recovery" masked unhealed chaos. He simply swapped one addiction for another.
He weaponized religion, turning "faith" into a tool of guilt and control.

Mic-Drop Truth

Faith without self-awareness is just another form of control.
No matter how shiny the Mercedes, you cannot outrun a stalled life.

Norman – When Normal Is Not Enough

(aka: Mr. Vanilla with No Sprinkles)

Meet Norman Gray. Even his name sounds like a yawn. Honestly, that is exactly what he was—the human equivalent of beige paint.

Norman was fine, pleasant, and safe. He had a good job, a master's in computer science, and worked for a solid tech company. He had no wild stories, no shady past, no drama. On paper, he was the guy you are supposed to want.

So why did I feel like I was slowly suffocating?

The Routine Robot

Here is the thing about Norman. His life ran on a clockwork hamster wheel. He made and ate the same breakfast, the same lunch, and the same dinner. He followed the same gym workout and went to bed at the same time every night.

He repeated everything, every single day.

Vacations? Nope. Sleeping in? Not allowed. Spontaneity? Absolutely not. He liked the world exactly as it was, always on repeat.

Even his house reflected the same pattern. It was a nice, good-sized place, but barely furnished. He kept a ping-pong table in the front room and a couple of random chairs in other rooms. It felt like he was half-living there, just enough to get by, but never fully invested.

That ping-pong table in his formal living room? It was a perfect metaphor for him: you could volley back and forth forever, but it never really went anywhere. It was just an endless, predictable bounce with no destination.

The Structured Fun

To his credit, Norman was not a bad man.

He could actually be fun: rollerblading down the Venice Boardwalk and coasting the San Diego hills on his Harley. We rollerbladed everywhere: Orange County and San Diego County paths, beach trails, even through Venice with crowds cheering as we zoomed by.

But the fun always came with a schedule. There was no, "Let's just hop on the bike and see where the day takes us." It was always, "We'll leave at 8 a.m., take this exact route, and be back by 11."

It was fun with a stopwatch.

Boring, But Sweet

He was nice, really nice. He was sweet in a steady, predictable way. He even invited my parents, who were visiting from out of town, over to his house for dinner one evening. What did he make?

The exact same dinner he made for himself every night: a piece of protein, a sweet potato (always a sweet potato, never a regular one), and a simple salad. It felt boring and basic, but it was thoughtful in its own way. My parents actually liked him. But thoughtful does not equal thrilling. It does not even equal interesting.

The Normal That Felt Numb

I dated him for 18 months, mostly because there was nothing technically wrong with him. There were no lies, no affairs, and no drama. But there was nothing exciting either.

The big "romantic gesture" he forgot? Valentine's Day. Not because he was cheating or scheming. He just did not think it mattered.

That is when I realized the problem. I wanted a man who felt something. Norman just existed.

The Breakup Line

When I finally broke it off, I told him the truth: "You're a subset of my much bigger world. I have so much more of the world I want to see and do, and you don't. You are content right here in this tiny box you have built for yourself. I cannot live in that box."

He blinked, shrugged, and said, "Okay."

That was it. There was no fight, no tears, no passion. It was just okay.

What I Should Have Noticed

If a man's biggest thrill is the same protein shake he has had for years, you are signing up for a lifetime of meh.
"Nice" is not the same as compatible.
Predictable is not always stable. Sometimes it is just stagnant.

Takeaway

Settling for safe can feel like a slow fade into invisibility.
You are not selfish for wanting a partner who excites your soul and steadies your life.
"Nice" is not enough when there is no spark, no depth, and no alignment with your values.

Lesson

Normal is not always safe. Sometimes it is just slowly draining.
Just because a man is stable does not mean he is your match.
Sometimes the man with no red flags still is not right, because life with him feels like it is stuck on repeat.
Norman taught me that safe is not always satisfying.

Red Flags to Remember

He was nice, but never truly present.
He avoided depth under the guise of keeping things "easy."
He made you question if you were asking for too much, when really, you were not asking for enough.

Mic-Drop Truth

Boring is not the same as peaceful. Settling for lukewarm love will leave you cold.
He was perfectly fine, so fine that he disappeared into the background like beige wallpaper.

Everett – The Trial Esquire

(aka: Mr. Meet Up)

Not every man I dated ended in a disaster. In fact, many never made it into this book. Those were the men I walked away from early, not because they did something awful or because there was a blowup or a fight, but because something felt off and I listened.

Those relationships faded quietly, without drama or confrontation. I just knew they were not right.

This story is one of those moments.

The First Meet Up

I met him in the desert while I was there with my girlfriends. He was visiting, passing through from Orange County, where I also had a home at the time. We struck up a conversation easily.

He was handsome, confident, and charming in a low-key way. He introduced himself as an "esquire," not a lawyer or an attorney. It felt less like a title and more like branding. It struck me as unusual, but also kind of amusing.

He gave me his card and asked me to reach out when I was back in town.

I did.

Always There, But Never Here

From the beginning, everything was about meeting up—lunch meetups, bike meetups, and boat meetups. We initially met for lunch, and it went well.

We discovered we both loved mountain biking, so we did that next. Then he invited me out on his boat and suggested I bring a friend. We spent the day on the water, dolphins riding the wake, sunshine, laughter. It felt magical.

After that, we went out on the boat many more times, just the two of us. We picnicked together. We drank wine and ate hors d'oeuvres.

We had those kinds of afternoons that feel romantic until you realize they never led anywhere. We anchored in the bay to watch the Newport Christmas boat parade. During other boat outings, I stayed on deck while he scuba dove.

We went shooting at the gun range. We were always laughing, always having fun. But I always met him there, whether it was at the marina, the dock, the trailhead, the gun range, or the restaurant.

He never picked me up. He never came to my house, nor was I ever invited to his.

When I asked why, he said he had a young son and shared custody with his ex. That explanation might have made sense, except it never quite added up. He did not have his son full-time, not even close. Still, his home remained completely off-limits.

Sick, But Not Vulnerable

Once, when he was sick, I offered to come over and take care of him. He refused. He said I might get sick too. That answer landed wrong. It was not concern. It was deflection.

There were other things that did not add up. The way he called me "honey" casually, like a habit already practiced. The way affection stayed light and distant. We rarely kissed, and when we did, it was brief and restrained.

There was no escalation, no deepening, and no movement forward.

That Dead Fish Smell

I asked directly if there was someone else in his life. He never answered the question. He simply let it fall into silence.

That was enough.

I did not need proof. I did not need a confession. I did not need to be right. Something smelled fishy, and I trusted myself.

I cut bait and let him go.

Always in Trial, Never Available

Later, when I started dating someone else, he resurfaced every few weeks with the same refrain. He was busy. He was in trial. "Let's meet up" was his mantra.

When he reached out again years later, I felt the same thing I had felt before. Nothing had changed. He denied there had ever been anyone else. I did not believe him, but more importantly, I no longer needed to.

Whatever the truth was did not matter. I did not want to live on the outside of a man's life. I did not want to be compartmentalized. I did not want partial access dressed up as privacy.

This was not a bad man. He was simply a misfit.

This time, I left when I knew.

What I Should Have Noticed

I was never invited into his real life.
Everything stayed contained, controlled, and separate.
Lack of access is information.

Takeaway

Discomfort without clarity is still a reason.
You do not need chaos to justify leaving.

Lesson

Trusting yourself does not require evidence.
It requires honesty with what you feel and the courage to act on it.

Red Flags to Remember

Deflection is the answer.
Stagnation is a choice.
A man who keeps you out of his home is keeping you out of something else.

Mic Drop Truth

Not all red flags wave wildly; some sit quietly and wait to see if you will abandon yourself.

This time, I did not.

SECTION VII: From Red Flags to Real Power – Your Guide to Trusting Yourself

This is where the stories stop being just cautionary tales and start becoming tools. This is where patterns become clarity, confusion turns into discernment, and you stop questioning your instincts and begin trusting them.

This section is not about bitterness, anger, or swearing off love. It is about real power. It is the kind of power that comes from knowing yourself so well that you stop negotiating with red flags or overriding your own intuition.

You do not have to repeat what I did. You can leave earlier. You can choose better. You can trust yourself the first time.

Teaser: "This is not just the end of bad dating. It is the beginning of your power."

When the Spotlight Turns Back on You

So, here we are.

You have ridden shotgun with me through every train-wreck relationship, dodging lies, cheap moves, giant egos, tiny—well, you know—and you have survived the parade of red flags right alongside me.

Now it is time to turn the spotlight away from them and back onto you.

Here is the thing. Spotting red flags is not really about them at all. It is about you: how willing you are to see what is right in front of you, how deeply you trust your gut, and how ready you are to walk away from the bullshit, even when it is wrapped in charm, muscles, money, or sweet words you want to believe.

This section is not a sermon. I am not here to tell you what you "should" do. I am here to give you the tools to understand why you tolerated what you tolerated, how to break the pattern for good, and how to become the kind of woman who does not even entertain this nonsense anymore.

From the smooth-talking cowboy con who rode in with charm but no substance, to the fake rockstar MD who played doctor on stage and in life, to the mountain-biking escape artist who left me running his business, and even Marvin, whose red flags were so blatant they might as well have been flashing neon right in front of me, every single one of them revealed the same truth.

My intuition whispered the warning signs early, and I overrode it with hope, excuses, and the fantasy of who they could be. Ignoring those whispers did not change the outcome; it only delayed it. That is the thing about red flags. They do not disappear. They only get louder the longer you refuse to see them.

Healing is not about finding the "right" man. It is about becoming the right woman for yourself.

Buckle up.

We are about to dig into the following:

Why we miss the red flags even when they are practically smacking us in the face
How to stop second-guessing your gut and begin trusting yourself
How to set non-negotiables and actually keep them
See the subtle emotional traps that keep you stuck
How to walk away without explaining yourself to anyone
How to rewrite your story so the next chapter is not another repeat

This is the part where we stop laughing at the insanity of my past and start learning how to honor your future. It is where you remember who you are.

Are you ready to drop the patterns, keep your crown straight, and trust yourself like never before?

Let us begin.

Why We Miss Red Flags

You know that gut feeling. The one that whispers, "Something feels off." Yeah, I ignored it over and over again.

Why? Because red flags rarely show up as giant neon signs flashing **RUN**. They arrive as subtle discomforts you push aside because you want the story to work.

Here is the uncomfortable truth. We do not miss red flags because we are foolish. We miss them because we are hopeful.

We want to believe the man who says, "I am just in between places right now," as if "temporary" comes with an expiration date. We want to believe the guy who swears his "crazy ex" is the reason he is struggling. We want to believe the charmer who promises, "This time I am serious."

Deep down, we want to believe we can be the one who finally makes it work.

The "Highlight Reel" Effect

In the beginning, they show you the best parts. They show you the charm, the smile, the sweet texts, the promises about the future, and sometimes even a little love bombing.

You are seeing a highlight reel, carefully edited for maximum appeal.

What you do not see right away are the missing scenes: the lies, the chaos, the half-truths, and occasionally, the hidden wife in the desert. (Yes, Sterling, I am looking at you.)

The Self-Doubt Trap

Then there is the voice in your head: maybe I am overthinking. Maybe I am being too picky. Maybe I just need to give him time.

You silence your gut and call it "being understanding." You label it patience, when it is actually fear—fear of being wrong, fear of being alone, or fear of starting over.

The Timing Factor

Here is another truth: red flag men have impeccable timing. They show up when you are vulnerable, stressed, lonely, exhausted, or quietly thinking, "I should probably get married by now."

They sense your uncertainty and slide in like a snake wearing a cowboy hat.

Why We Stay Even When We Know

Even when the lies begin to unravel, we stay a little longer because we have already invested. We have told our friends. We have already imagined the life.

Sometimes, admitting we were wrong feels harder than pretending everything is fine.

Take Grant, the Trophy Titan.

The night he took me to my birthday dinner, I wore a wig as part of a fun little game I loved playing with my girlfriends called "Wigging Out." I thought he would laugh. I thought he would find it playful.

Instead, he became irritated.

He called me selfish for wearing it. He said, "I was getting to know a blonde, and now you're confusing me with this brunette thing." Then he claimed his friends agreed it was strange.

I should have walked out of that restaurant, but I did not. I removed the wig. I shrank myself to accommodate a man who could not handle one night of lighthearted fun.

Remember Tom, the Trailer Park Charmer whose red flags did not whisper? They waved repeatedly.

His issue was not cruelty. It was emotional entanglement, and familiarity disguised as loyalty and intimacy. He kept long-standing connections alive, blurred boundaries without apology, and treated proximity like proof of closeness.

He said the right things, including "I choose you" and "I have your back."

He delivered those words convincingly, appearing sincere and present, embodying the man I hoped he could be. However, his actions told a different story.

He chose comfort over growth, familiarity over depth, and motion over presence. He assumed access instead of earning connection and mistook time spent together for emotional attunement.

I stayed longer than I should have because I was not just dating who he was; I was dating who he could be. I was dating the potential and the version of him that showed up in flashes. This was the version I hoped would finally settle into consistency if I was patient enough.

Yes, the dancing helped blur the truth. It felt connective. It felt electric. It felt like chemistry. But, chemistry without clarity is just another way to postpone the obvious.

I did not miss the red flags. I talked myself out of them.

Then there was Brandy, the Liquor Liar. At a dinner party I hosted, he arrived hours late. One of my friends confronted him immediately, "You've got another woman, don't you?"

He deflected with, "Who are you to talk to me like this?"

Instead of standing in the truth that already sat in my gut, I stayed silent. I seated him, served him, and let the moment pass because admitting it publicly felt heavier than denial.

Later, the pieces aligned. My friend had been right.

Mic-Drop Truth

Your intuition does not lie. Your fear does.
The real work is learning to trust yourself enough to walk away the first time something feels off, before the excuses multiply and before the lies mature into disasters.
A red flag is not a puzzle to decode; it is a boundary to honor.

Breaking the Pattern – Why the Universe Keeps Sending You the Same Partner

Here is the truth that stings a little. If you do not heal the wound, you will keep choosing the same bandage. He will be a different name and a different face, but the same damn story.

I know this because it happened to me.

Clay was my first "cowboy con." Colt was the sequel. He wore the same boots and the same swagger, but he was a bigger and more convincing liar. At the time, I told myself, *This one is different.* He seemed more successful, more stable, and more ready.

He was not. The part that matters most is this: it was not about them.

It was about me.

The Psychology of Attraction & Familiar Wounds

We are wired to seek the familiar, even when familiar is toxic.

If you grew up with chaos, you may unconsciously crave a man who creates chaos. If you learned that love had to be earned, you will be drawn to men who make you work for every drop of affection.

Your nervous system confuses what is familiar with what is safe.

This is why you can walk right past a good, steady man who would never lie to you and fall headfirst for the charming liar who feels like "home."

The universe, life, God, whatever name fits, keeps sending the same archetype until you finally recognize the lesson. It is not meant to punish you. It is meant to wake you up.

When My Gut Screamed & I Still Ignored It

Patterns do not break quietly. They start as whispers. There are small nudges, subtle discomfort, and flickers of unease that you can rationalize away. If you ignore them long enough, they grow louder. Eventually, your body steps in when your mind refuses to listen.

With Clay, the whispers came early. My gut said something is off. I was young, stressed, and trying to be kind:

Do not be cruel.
He has been through a lot.
Maybe he just needs support.

I silenced my intuition because it felt "kinder."

With Colt, the pattern did not whisper. It screamed.

The night before I married him, I cried uncontrollably. It was not nerves or jitters. It was something deeper. I remember wiping my face and trying to talk myself out of what I was feeling:

Everyone gets cold feet.
People have flown in.
I have already set this whole thing in motion.

I pushed my intuition down again and walked right into a marriage that would become a nightmare. The Universe does not let you ignore yourself forever.

After three years in that marriage, I was already planning my escape and uncovering the lies. Even then, I had not fully allowed myself to admit the truth.

Then my body made the decision for me.

A deep nausea hit, as if my stomach was collapsing inward. I fell to my knees. My vision blurred and everything darkened at the edges. Heat rose from my core into my chest, my throat, and my head.

It was not panic. It was clarity. In that moment, I finally admitted the truth I had been running from:

I had been lied to.
I had been duped.
If I did not save myself, I was going to disappear.

It was terrifying, and it was the first time I truly listened.

Healing Changes What You Are Attracted to

Once you start to heal those wounds, something incredible happens:

Men like Clay, Colt, or Damian stop looking appealing. Their chaos feels loud instead of magnetic. Their love bombing feels intrusive rather than exciting. Their "mystery" feels exhausting instead of alluring.

Healing sharpens your radar. You see the lies faster, spot inconsistencies sooner, and feel the emotional void instead of decorating it with fantasy. You stop being compatible with what once hurt you.

Why Familiar Feels So Seductive

So why do we stay with men we already know are not right? On some level, it feels like home.

If home was unstable, instability feels "normal." If love was conditional, proving yourself feels "romantic." If you were the fixer, the helper, or the emotional anchor, you will find men who expect you to carry it all.

We repeat patterns because they are familiar and familiar feels safer than the unknown, even when that unknown is where healing lives.

Journal Prompts to Break Your Pattern

- Take a deep breath, grab a pen, and get honest with yourself.
- What did "love" feel like in your childhood home? (Were you walking on eggshells, experiencing conditional love, or feeling ignored?)
- What familiar emotional dynamic have you repeated in relationships?
- When you think of the men who hurt you most, what do they have in common? (Were they charming, unstable, controlling, or emotionally unavailable?)
- How did you feel in those relationships? (Did you feel small, overlooked, or as if you had to prove yourself?)
- What would a calm, consistent relationship feel like to you? (Does it feel comforting or does it feel boring?)
- Write it all down and sit with it. When you can see the pattern clearly, you finally hold the power to break it.

Mic-Drop Truth

The universe does not keep sending you the same man because it hates you. It sends him because you have not learned to choose differently.

106

Stop trying to fix the man in front of you and start fixing the part of you that let him in.

Non-Negotiables – Defining What You Will Never Compromise Again

Here is one of the hardest lessons I learned. Every time you compromise your core values, you teach someone how to mistreat you.

For a long time, I thought I had non-negotiables. I did not. Worse, I bent them the moment someone charming asked me to.

I ignored the small things that made me cringe. I told myself they were not that bad. I hid behind phrases like, "No one's perfect" or "I am probably being too picky."

Here is the truth: red flags never stay small. They grow.

Why Non-Negotiables Matter

Non-negotiables are your personal dealbreakers. They are not shallow preferences like "he must be 6' 2" or "he needs a six-pack." They are the values, behaviors, and life choices that, when crossed, slowly erode your self-respect and peace.

When you are clear on them, you stop wasting time on men who were never going to align with you anyway.

When you are not clear, you start rationalizing why it is acceptable that he lies about small things, neglects his health or hygiene, cannot manage his life or hold steady work, or does not treat you the way you want and deserve to be treated.

Ask me how I know.

When I Ignored My Non-Negotiables

Here we go...

I always said I would never date a smoker. I hated the smell, and I hated what it said about how someone treated their body.

Yet, I did.

Grant, the Trophy Titan turned Therapy Project, hid his smoking at first. On the surface, he was a polished, country-club athlete, showcasing tennis, health, and discipline. Behind closed doors, he chain-smoked and hid it from everyone.

I should have left the first time I smelled it on him. Instead, I told myself, *It is just a small thing. I am probably overreacting. He has so many other good qualities.*

Then came Marvin, "Starvin' Marvin," the Human Ashtray. He did not just smoke. He left behind piles of ash, yellowed fingers, and that stale, suffocating smell everywhere. I still stayed too long, even after he invited me on a "vacation" to Hawaii and made me pay for my own damn food.

Looking back, I cringe.

I knew smoking was a non-negotiable for me. I ignored it because I was afraid of being "too picky."

Here is the part no one tells you. The longer you stay, the harder it becomes to leave.

The Cost of Lowering My Bar

Then there was Tom, the Trailer Park Charmer. He would sit in the driver's seat and pick his nose while we drove for hours. It sounds funny now, but in the moment, I remember thinking,

Did he really just do that?
Did I really just lower my bar this far?

Worse, I lowered it repeatedly.

I excused Colt's lies because I "wanted to believe in love."
I overlooked Damian's fake PhD because he made me laugh.
I rationalized Johnny the Outlaw's booty-call behavior because it was fun in the moment.

Every time I ignored a non-negotiable, I chipped away at my own self-trust. Once fractured, self-trust is difficult to rebuild.

How to Create Your Own Non-Negotiables

If you want to stop repeating the same relationships, you have to get radically honest, not about what you want, but about what you will no longer tolerate.

Ask yourself:

- What patterns caused me the most pain?
- When did I feel small, drained, or invisible?
- What have I repeatedly excused that I cannot excuse again?

Your list might sound like this:

- I will not date a man who lies.
- I will not date a man who neglects his health.
- I will not date a man without integrity or follow-through.
- I will not date a man who disrespects my time, energy, or boundaries.

Then comes the part most people skip. You stick to it.

If you bend once, you will bend again. Before you know it, you are years into something you knew from day one was not right.

The Three-Month, Six-Month & Nine-Month Rule

One boundary that changed everything for me is what I call the Three-Month, Six-Month, and yes, the Nine-Month Rule.

The Three-Month Rule is your observation period. You do not rush intimacy or build future fantasies. You watch, listen, and notice whether his words match his actions. Does he show up consistently, or does he only talk pretty when it is convenient? Time reveals patterns when you let it. After three months, you should have a clear sense of whether he is worth continuing down the path with you.

The Six-Month Rule is your reality checkpoint. You step back and ask yourself whether you feel calm and secure, or whether you are already explaining away things that do not sit right because you do not want to start over.

After six months, reevaluate. Do I see a future here? Are there red flags I am glossing over? Am I growing or quietly shrinking?

Then there is the Nine-Month Rule. This is for relationships that look almost right but still are not right.

He says he is choosing you, but his behavior does not fully align. He keeps options open, blurs boundaries, or asks for patience while offering breadcrumbs.

Nine months is more than generous. If you are still negotiating your needs, waiting for consistency, or explaining away hurt at that point, that is your cue to get the hell out.

That is exactly what happened to me in one relationship. My gut knew from the very beginning that I should not have dated him. I saw the red flags early. I followed the Three-Month Rule. I honored the Six-Month Rule. By the nine-month mark, I finally chose myself.

I did not leave because he failed to say he was choosing me. He did. I left because his actions never aligned with his words.

When I walked away, the patterns I had questioned did not stop. They repeated themselves exactly as my intuition had warned me they would.

This rule is not about catching someone doing something wrong. It is about stopping yourself from settling for "almost" when your body already knows the truth.

Three months to observe.
Six months to assess.
Nine months to choose yourself.

Anything beyond that is not hope. It is crumbs.

Had I enforced this rule earlier, Damian's lies would have smacked me in the face sooner. Colt's cracks would have been clear as day. Maxwell's illusions would have shattered before I ever bought the fantasy. Tom's blurred boundaries and rotating orbit of women would have been enough for me to remove myself immediately.

What I Should Have Noticed

Looking back, it is painfully clear:

The first cringe moment is always a preview of more to come.
The first excuse you make becomes the breaking point.

The moment you say, "It is not that bad," is the moment you should walk away.

Your body knows. Your gut knows. Your non-negotiables exist to protect that knowing.

Mic-Drop Truth

Every time you ignore your non-negotiables, you betray yourself.
A man who smokes when you cannot stand it is not your man.
A man who lies when you value honesty is not your man.
A man who disrespects your boundaries the first time will do it again.
He is showing you who he is. Believe him because if you do not hold your standards, no one else will.

Rebuilding Your Self-Trust

When you have been burned by lies, betrayal, or repeated disappointment, trusting yourself again can feel impossible. You begin to second-guess everything.

Was I overreacting?
Did I imagine it?
Was I too picky?

Here is the truth. Losing trust in men is painful. Losing trust in yourself is far worse.

The good news is that self-trust can be rebuilt.

Start Small: Listen to Your Gut on the Little Things

When you have spent years overriding your intuition, you have to retrain it like a muscle.

If you get a strange vibe from someone you just met, notice it.
If you feel exhausted after a conversation, honor that.
If something feels "off," even if you cannot explain it yet, do not dismiss it.

Listening to yourself in small moments builds the strength to trust yourself when it matters most.

Boundaries Are Proof You Have Got Your Own Back

The most powerful way to rebuild self-trust is by keeping promises to yourself.

If you say, "I am not dating smokers anymore," then do not.
If you say, "I am leaving when I see the first lie," then mean it.

Boundaries are not walls. They are filters. They protect your energy so you have space for what actually nourishes you.

Release the Shame

This part matters more than most people realize. You have to stop punishing yourself for falling for it.

Here is the truth. You did not fall for the man. You fell for the hope of who he could be. You hoped he was who he claimed to be, and you hoped this time would be different.

That does not make you foolish. It makes you human.

The Self-Trust Reset

Write down every time your gut was right, even when you ignored it.

Pay attention to how your body warned you, whether it showed up as tightness in your chest, a pit in your stomach, or sleepless nights. Then make a simple commitment to yourself: the next time your body speaks, you will listen.

Trust is not rebuilt overnight. It is rebuilt through consistent, small choices to honor yourself again and again.

A Personal Reminder: Your Body Knows Before Your Mind Admits It

I will never forget the day my body finally gave out during my marriage to Colt, the Texas Sequel & Marriage Nightmare. I had ignored my intuition for years.

I ignored the crying fits before the wedding, and I ignored the steady drips of lies that kept piling up.

The day I finally admitted to myself that I needed to leave, my body collapsed.

It began with a deep sinking in my stomach, as if I was about to vomit. My vision blurred, and my knees gave way. Heat rushed from my core up my neck, burning into my head. I felt as if my body was screaming for me to finally listen.

That is the power of your gut. It starts by whispering. If you keep silencing it, it eventually screams.

Gaslighters rely on this disconnect. They are skilled at making you feel irrational for even questioning them.

Damian, the Music Man Who Played Doctor, was a perfect example. My gut knew his PhD story did not add up. When I finally confronted him over lunch, he leaned back, smiled, and said in a patronizing tone, "Oh honey, of course I have a PhD. I went to the University of Phoenix online. You are just overthinking."

He made me feel foolish for asking, as if I was the problem for questioning his credentials. When I saw another woman, an actual psychologist, believe him and even feature him on her radio show, my self-doubt deepened.

If she believes him, maybe I am wrong. Maybe I am just being too suspicious. No, I was not wrong. I just did not trust myself enough to hold the line.

Then there was Sterling, the Married Millionaire. At one of his homes in PGA West, he gave me the full bachelor-pad tour. When we stepped into the master bedroom, I froze. The closet was full of women's clothes, and the bathroom counter was lined with products that were clearly hers. I asked why everything was still there.

He barely reacted. "Oh, she just uses this place sometimes for girlfriend weekends. I let her. I have plenty of other houses to stay in, so it is no big deal."

Instead of honoring what my gut was screaming, that this situation was not normal for a man claiming to be divorcing, I swallowed the feeling. I allowed his explanation to override my truth.

That is the trap. They offer a story that sounds just believable enough for you to silence yourself because you do not want to lose the fantasy you have already invested in.

Mic-Drop Truth

The most trustworthy person you will ever meet should be you.
When you rebuild your self-trust, you stop second-guessing yourself, stop tolerating excuses, and start listening to the one voice that never lies: your own.

Dating with Clarity & Confidence

Once you have rebuilt your self-trust, the next step is learning how to date without losing yourself in the process.

After you have been burned, it is tempting to swing to extremes. You either build walls so high no one can get through, or you throw the gates wide open for the first man who shows you a little attention. Neither approach works.

Dating with clarity and confidence requires balance. It means staying open to love while remaining fiercely loyal to yourself first.

Know Who You Are Before You Let Someone In

Most women start dating backwards. They go in asking whether he is the one. The better question is whether you are showing up as your most grounded and authentic self.

If you do not know your values, your boundaries, or the kind of partnership you truly want, you will get swept into someone else's life. You will adapt to his schedule, his dreams, and his timeline, and one day you will realize that you disappeared in the process.

Clarity comes from knowing yourself well enough to recognize immediately when someone does not align with you.

Recognize Genuine Emotional Availability

How do you tell the difference between someone who is emotionally available and someone who is simply love-bombing you?

An emotionally available person respects your time and energy without rushing the process. He is consistent in his words and actions. He can talk about his past without blaming everyone else. He asks you about your dreams, your fears, and your needs.

Love-bombers dazzle you at the beginning, but they cannot sustain depth. Emotionally available partners build trust slowly and steadily, without chaos or drama.

Protect Your Energy While Staying Open

Protecting your energy does not mean closing off. It means filtering.

If someone shows a red flag, you pause and reassess instead of making excuses. If your gut feels uneasy, you step back and observe what he does rather than what he says. If someone crosses a boundary early, you do not rationalize it. You leave.

You cannot control how someone else shows up, but you always control how long you stay. Theory does not matter if you do not apply it in real life.

Here is what it looks like when you do not protect your energy:
I think about the trip I took to Hawaii with Marvin "Starvin' Marvin," the Pus-Picking Human Ashtray. My gut knew the relationship was over before we even boarded the flight. I felt the tightness in my chest and the sickness in my stomach. My body already knew it was done.

I stayed anyway. I had already split the cost of the flight and hotel, and I did not want to cause a scene or deal with the conflict of leaving him there. So, I shut down my intuition, went on the trip, and focused on finding fun things to do without him just to get through it. I ignored my body's screaming, *Leave now,* and waited until we got home to end it.

Here is what it looks like when you do protect your energy:

Think about Vinny the Mobster in Disguise, who told me he had part of his intestine removed after a mild cancer scare. His doctor gave him strict dietary instructions, and I watched him ignore every one of them. He ate sushi, red meat, carbohydrates, and drank alcohol, all of which he had been told to avoid.

When he became very sick one day, I brought him electrolytes, echinacea, and other healthy things he requested. As I left his house, I realized this was a man who did not take care of himself, and I was not willing to become his nurse.

When he called a few days later to make plans, I told him the truth. I explained that it was not going to work for me because he was not taking care of his health, and I could not be with someone who would not take responsibility for himself.

That was the end of it. I did not drag it out or ignore my instincts. There was no drama, no overexplaining, and no self-betrayal. I set a clean, confident boundary.

Walking away at two months felt powerful. It was proof that I no longer needed to stay and fix someone.

Here is the difference:

When you ignore your gut, like I did with Marvin, you leave drained, resentful, and ashamed you did not listen sooner.

When you honor your gut, like I did with Vinny, you leave early, clean, and free, without losing your energy or yourself.

The Queen Test

Ask yourself after every date:

- Did I feel seen and heard, or did I feel like I had to prove my worth?
- Did I leave with more energy or less?
- Did I feel calm in his presence, or did my body feel tense and guarded?

Dating with clarity is not about finding perfection. It is about recognizing alignment and trusting yourself enough to walk away when it is not there.

Reflection Questions for Dating with Clarity & Confidence

- What did past relationships cost you in terms of energy, time, or self-respect?
- How did you feel in your body during those relationships, whether light and expansive or heavy and drained?
- Where have you ignored a red flag to "keep the peace" or avoid conflict?
- What would it have looked like to honor yourself instead?
- What are your current non-negotiables?
- Which behaviors are a hard no?
- Which behaviors are essential for alignment?
- Do you leave dates feeling empowered or questioning yourself?
- What does your body tell you after spending time with someone new?
- What would it look like to protect your energy while staying open?
- How can you stay curious about someone without abandoning your own needs or boundaries?

Mic-Drop Truth

You are not auditioning for a man's love. He is revealing whether he is worthy of yours.

The Queen Energy Reset

There is a moment, after heartbreak and self-blame, when you finally realize that you were never asking for too much. You were just asking the wrong men. This is the turning point: the shift from wounded to empowered, and from begging for crumbs to embodying the energy of a woman who knows she deserves the whole damn feast.

Here is the truth:

A Queen does not chase.
A Queen does not explain her worth.
A Queen does not shrink herself to fit someone else's story.
A Queen sits in her power, and the right people, including friends, lovers, and opportunities, align with her.

Returning to Your Own Power

Before you can attract something healthy, you have to remember who you are without the noise of everyone else's needs.

This process begins with your body:

You move your body in ways that remind you it belongs to you.
You dance, walk, stretch, and take up space without apology.
You dress in a way that makes you feel alive rather than hidden.
You reconnect with the version of yourself that existed before the lies dimmed your light.

It also begins with your energy:

You stop engaging with people and situations that consistently drain you. You redirect your focus toward what lights you up, including your goals, passions, and peace.

You release the belief that you "wasted time" on the wrong men. You did not waste time. You learned.

The Queen Walk

I created a simple but powerful reset while rebuilding myself. I call it the Queen Walk.

- Pick a song that makes you feel confident, bold, and grounded.
- Put on an outfit that makes you feel good, even if you are staying home.
- Walk across the room slowly and deliberately with your chin lifted. Allow your body to take up space as your energy expands.

Your hips are your throne.

That sacred space, which includes your sacrum, womb, and creative center, is not just physical. It is energetic. It is where life begins, ideas are born, and your capacity to create and nurture life resides. This space is the wellspring of feminine power.

When you walk with your hips leading, you allow that energy to move through you. Your body opens, and your power grounds itself into each step.

Take this walk beyond your living room. Walk into your workplace this way. Walk through the grocery store this way. Walk into your favorite coffee shop this way. Walk into the next date this way.

When your energy flows from your center, people notice. They feel it before you speak, and they respond to it instinctively.

Watch out. The Queen has arrived.

Sounds simple or silly? Try it.

You will feel the shift in minutes. It is a physical reminder that you belong in every room you enter, without shrinking and without apologizing.

How I Discovered the Queen Walk for Myself

The Queen Walk emerged after my breakup with Sterling, the Married Millionaire. I left him, but the relationship still left me gutted. I believe there had been a deep connection, but the truth was that I was recognizing pieces of myself in him.

I needed a way to rebuild my self-worth and reclaim my space.

It began playfully. My girlfriends and I wore wigs, dressed as alter egos, and went out embodying lighter, braver versions of ourselves. We called it *Wigging Out*, and it became our own hysterical little ritual. We did this at the Palm Desert nightclubs, and it made us feel alive again. We laughed until our sides hurt, flirted with life instead of men, and reminded ourselves what it felt like to walk into a room without shrinking. The stories we could tell and the fun we shared were priceless, and honestly, those nights did more for my healing than half the serious conversations I had been having with myself.

Something deeper clicked for me after that. I realized this was not really about wigs or costumes. It was about stepping into Queen energy intentionally, about owning my throne, my sacred sacrum-center, and the seat of my power. *Wigging Out* was simply the doorway. What mattered was how I carried myself once I stepped through it.

When I focused on that space, my shoulders relaxed and my hands opened, with my palms slightly turned outward. I allowed my hips to lead as I walked, slowly and intentionally, the same way I describe in the Queen Walk. Sometimes I wore heels, and sometimes I wore jeans. The clothes did not matter. The energy did, and when I moved through the world from that place, I started to see the results.

I carried that walk everywhere. I brought it into boardrooms, errands, restaurants, and everyday moments. People responded differently.

One night in the desert, a friend and I walked into a popular music and dance spot with no reservation and no plan. We were dressed confidently and held ourselves like we belonged there. Our heads were high, and our hips led the way. The maître d' motioned us over immediately and seated us in the VIP section. We did not ask. The energy spoke first.

Experiences like that repeated themselves. When you carry yourself like a Queen, with grounded confidence, the world adjusts.

Exercise to Reconnect with Your Worth

This exercise changed everything for me:

- Write down your non-negotiables in love and life, and then read them out loud as a vow to yourself.
- Make a list of your wins, including moments when you honored your intuition, overcame something difficult, or stood tall when it felt uncomfortable.
- Create a daily mantra that reminds you of who you are.
  (Mine was simple and direct. I am not a rehabilitation center for broken men. I am a whole woman deserving of a whole love.)

The New Standard

The Queen Energy Reset is not about superiority. It is about refusing to live beneath your own worth.

When you embody this energy, you stop being impressed by bare minimum effort. You stop confusing chaos with passion. You stop overexplaining why you are leaving situations that do not feel right. You simply walk away without apology.

Mic-Drop Truth

A Queen does not fear being alone. She fears dimming her crown for the wrong man.

You Are Not Broken, You Are Becoming Unshakable

Here is something no one tells you when you are sifting through the wreckage of another relationship that did not work. You are not broken. You are not "too much." You are not doomed to repeat the same story forever.

You are becoming.

Every red flag you ignored, every gut feeling you silenced, and every tear you cried in the dark taught you something. Those lessons may have bruised your heart, but they did not destroy it. They sharpened it. They forced you to see what you had been unwilling to see before.

After walking through all of this myself, I can tell you this with certainty: the goal is not to build higher walls. The goal is not to become cold or bitter. The goal is to become unshakable.

What Unshakable Actually Means

Unshakable does not mean untouchable. It does not mean you stop feeling or stop loving.

It means you know your worth well enough that you no longer trade it for crumbs. It means you see red flags and respect what they are without trying to decode or excuse them. It means you understand the difference between a man's potential and his reality, and you stop trying to build a future on who he might someday become.

It means you trust your intuition. It means you walk into a room grounded in who you are. It means love becomes a choice you make from strength, not a rescue mission you sign up for out of hope.

The Shift That Changes Everything

When you finally see yourself clearly, something sacred shifts.

You stop auditioning for approval. You stop questioning whether you are "enough." You stop chasing men who cannot meet you and begin choosing men who can.

You stop fearing solitude.

Being alone is not lonely when you respect the woman you are becoming. Calm replaces chaos. Discernment replaces desperation. Love begins to flow from abundance rather than lack.

The Truth to Carry with You

Every time you doubted yourself, you were still worthy. Every time you stayed too long, you were still worthy. Even when you gave parts of yourself to men who could not hold them well, you were still whole.

You do not have to "fix" yourself before love shows up. You do not need to "earn" a healthy relationship. You need to remember who you are and refuse to abandon her again.

Mic-Drop Truth

You are not broken. You are a masterpiece in motion. You are becoming unshakable.
Heartbreak did not ruin you. It clarified you.
Wear your crown because it belongs to you, not because you are waiting for someone else to notice it.

SECTION VIII: The Integration – Where the Lessons Become Your Life

This is where everything you have learned stops being theory and starts becoming instinct. You are no longer just spotting red flags or breaking patterns. You are living differently. Self-trust no longer feels like something you have to force. Your standards are not rules you have to fight to enforce. They are simply who you are now.

This section reflects what happens after the wake-up calls, when the lesson finally becomes your life. Clarity replaces confusion. You stop explaining yourself to people who cannot meet you where you are, and you stop negotiating with what you already know. This is not about closure for the past. It is about alignment with the woman you have become.

Teaser: "This is what it looks like when you stop dating red flags and start living from your truth."

The Saturn Return Season

This was never only about the men. It was the cycle I kept living inside.

I have always believed there is a rhythm to our becoming. The ancients tracked it. The mystics named it. Some call it timing, and others call it karma. The astrologers call it a Saturn Return, a sacred season of life that demands you confront yourself, get honest, and stop repeating what is not working. Saturn is known as the taskmaster, the planet of responsibility and reckoning. It does not punish. It assigns the lesson you have been avoiding and waits for you to rise.

Even if you do not follow astrology, you know this moment. Life starts stripping away what is not true. You feel pressure. You feel clarity. You feel the same lesson showing up again, and you realize you cannot talk your way around it anymore.

The first Saturn Return hits in your late twenties to early thirties. Mine came at twenty-nine, and I got married. By thirty-two, it was over.

That was my first Saturn fire, and it burned through illusion and identity. It dismantled what I thought I was supposed to do and forced me to face what I had been ignoring.

I thought I had learned the lesson, and I believed the cycle was complete. That belief did not hold.

In the months leading up to my second Saturn Return, the ground started shifting again. A man showed up. A pattern reappeared. A choice stood right in front of me.

This time, the decision was not about building a life with someone. This time, the decision was about reclaiming my own.

This is what the second Saturn Return required. It required truth at a level I could not negotiate with or soften for comfort.

The relationships in this book were not random. They were patterns I had to see clearly. Each man reflected something back to me, and each heartbreak forced a decision about what I would tolerate, what I would excuse, and what I would keep abandoning in myself.

The man I walked away from most recently was not just another red flag. He was a test of whether I would repeat the cycle or finally stop participating in it.

That moment was not only a breakup. It was a reckoning. It was the point where I stopped orbiting someone else's gravity and returned to my own center.

This is what Saturn does when you are ready. It gets loud. It removes distractions. It exposes the stories you have been living on. It leaves you with the truth and asks what you are going to do with it.

I did not come here to settle for "almost." I did not come here to shrink myself to fit what someone else could offer. I did not come here to keep learning the same lesson through different men.

This season was not just the end of a relationship. It was the end of who I had to be to survive. It was the beginning of who I am becoming to thrive.

If you are standing in the wreckage of something you thought would last, hear this clearly. You are not falling apart. You are waking up.

You might call it Saturn. You might call it timing. You might call it the universe forcing your hand.

I call it the moment you finally get yourself back. This is your return.

Reflection Invitation: Your Saturn Season

This is not a chapter you read quickly. It is a chapter that completes something if you let it.

If you feel called, sit with these questions:

- What pattern has followed you across time and still wants to be broken?
- What belief about love keeps pulling you back into the same kind of pain?
- Who are you when you stop orbiting someone else and return to your own life?

Let your answers come slowly. Let them be honest. Let them lead you back to yourself.

The Message I Sent Anyway

I told myself I would not send it. I told myself I was done and that the words were better left unsaid. Grief does not always follow rules, and clarity does not always arrive in silence.

So yes, I sent the message.

I had ended it. I had walked away on purpose, on principle, with every ounce of strength I had. Still, I opened my heart one more time. I was not begging, and I was not bargaining. I needed to say what was still sitting in my chest.

Part of me questioned the decision. I wondered whether I had just reopened something I worked hard to close.

Here is what I understand now.

I did not need his reply. I needed my own clarity.

The moment after I sent it, something settled. I saw the pattern clearly. I was still reaching toward someone who had never reached back. I was still hoping crumbs would finally feel like enough. I was still trying to rewrite a story that had already ended.

That realization did not shame me. It clarified me.

I forgave myself for feeling. I forgave myself for loving. I forgave myself for reaching one last time.

Healing is rarely a straight line. Sometimes it circles back just far enough to show you how much you have grown. The difference this time was not that I sent the message. The difference was that I did not abandon myself afterward. I did not chase. I did not negotiate. I did not shrink. I listened.

When I sent messages like that in the past, I was asking someone to choose me. This time, I was asking myself whether I still needed him.

The answer was no.

The Reckoning & the Awakening

This is where a woman's real life begins.

It does not begin when someone chooses her. It does not begin with a ring or the illusion that she finally "got it right." It begins in the quiet after the storm, when she is standing in the ashes of everything she once hoped would work and realizes she is still here: still breathing, still hurting, and still standing, but no longer begging.

It begins the moment she says, "No more," and means it. It begins when she decides that she will no longer abandon herself to stay chosen.

This is the reckoning. It is the reckoning of every lie she believed, every standard she lowered, and every piece of herself she handed over to men who could not hold it.

I have to be honest with myself.

I have thrown red flags too. I was not always the hero in someone else's story. I stayed too long and sometimes left too quickly. I played the fixer. I confused chemistry with compatibility. I treated my worth like it was negotiable. There were moments when I was someone else's red flag.

That truth matters.

Awareness is where the pattern finally breaks. I do not need to be perfect to be powerful. I need to be honest. The woman who owns her patterns is the woman who rewrites them.

I did not write this book to drag exes or position myself as a victim. I wrote it to crawl out of the wreckage of my own choices. I wrote it to face the truth without softening it. I wrote it to sit with the shame long enough to understand it, and then refuse to live there.

This is the turning point. This is where I reclaim my worth and stop negotiating with it.

If you are holding onto someone who keeps dimming your light, you already know it. If you are twisting yourself to stay chosen, you feel it in your body. If you are waiting for someone else to rise before you do, you are delaying your own life.

Rise anyway.

The woman you are becoming is not a beggar. She is not a backup plan. She is not collecting red flags like souvenirs from lessons she refuses to finish.

She is finished learning the same lesson. She is choosing herself. She is rewriting the story.

Reader Reflection Prompt: The Reckoning Within

This is not about who hurt you. It is about what you are no longer willing to tolerate.

Ask yourself:

- Where have I been silencing myself to keep the peace?
- What parts of me have I been shrinking to stay in someone else's story?
- Who am I without this pain?
- What would it look like to choose myself without apology or delay?
- If I stopped settling today, what would I begin claiming?

136

Write your reckoning. Say it out loud. Let it become something you act on.

This is where your new story begins.

How to Stop Dating Red Flags (For Real)

I did not write this book while wrapped up in someone else's arms. I wrote it after I walked away for good. I wrote it once the lesson was learned, not while I was still negotiating it. I chose myself.

This book is not just a collection of cautionary tales and wild red-flag stories. It is catharsis. It is reclamation. It is truth.

It holds every version of me who handed herself away too easily to the unavailable, the self-absorbed, and the emotionally lazy. It holds the woman who mistook charm for character and confusion for connection, including the charming liars who wore red flags like designer cologne.

These pages were written after I peeled back outdated beliefs and confronted the stories I told myself just to keep the wrong men a little longer.

No, I am not in a relationship as I finish this.

What I am in is something far more sacred: alignment with myself, alignment with truth, and alignment with the kind of love I will never fight to earn.

I know the difference now between chemistry and compatibility, between being chosen and being cherished, between attention and intention, and between a man who speaks beautifully and a man who shows up.

I do not need perfect. I need present. I do not need constant fireworks. I need steady fire.

You met the cowboys, the charmers, the scammers, the smokers, the liars, the tiny pencil peckers, and the giant egos with the zip-code-sized dongs. You laughed. You cringed. You have probably whispered, "Oh hell, I dated that guy too."

Here is what matters. You are not broken. You were learning.

Every wrong turn, every late-night cry, every "How did I end up here?" moment was pointing you back to yourself.

You do not need a fixer-upper. You do not need crumbs. You do not need a man who makes you doubt your worth. You deserve the whole damn feast.

You do not earn that feast by shrinking, over-giving, or twisting yourself into something "easier" to love. You claim it by owning your space, trusting your gut, and walking away from chaos without explaining yourself.

This book is not about ending relationships. It is about ending self-abandonment.

The real love story here was never about him. It was about you returning to yourself, refusing to dim your light, and finally trusting that your intuition is smarter than your hope.

If you are reading this thinking, "That is me," take this as permission. Say goodbye if you need to. Close the door if you must. Choose yourself without apology.

Wear your standards like stilettos and your wisdom like war paint. If you ever set your crown down just to survive him, go back and pick it up. Wear it with strength and clarity. Wear it because it is yours.
The next chapter is not about red flags. It is about you.

This time, you write it.

The Final Mic-Drop Truth

The crown was never theirs to give you. It was yours all along.

The Night Before the Rise

You made it through the book. You nodded. You laughed. You winced. You underlined sentences and whispered, "God, I've been there."

Then comes the night.

It is quiet. It aches. It is the kind of night when you stare at your phone a little longer than you should. It is the kind of night where absence feels louder than the wisdom you just gained. It is the kind of night where the past begins to look softer than it really was.

This is the night before the rise.

If you find yourself there, do not panic. Do not shame yourself. Do not mistake the ache for weakness. It is not failure. It is the final tug of an old pattern that no longer fits you.

Growth is rarely loud. It is often quiet and uncomfortable. Sometimes it looks like sitting on your bed, resisting the urge to reach back toward something you already know was not enough.

Even strong women have moments of doubt. Even healed women have nights where the old story tries to rewrite itself.

Breathe.

Hold the part of you that almost reached out. Speak gently to the version of you who once would have. Tell her, "I choose us now."

This is not the fall. It is the pause before you stand taller than you have before.

When morning comes, you will still be a Queen.

Tomorrow, you rise.

CROWN ON.

About the Author

Karen A. Dahlman, MA, is a psychotherapist, author, international speaker, and recognized researcher in the study of human behavior and consciousness. With a Master's degree in Art Psychotherapy and advanced training in hypnosis, regression work, and counseling, she has spent decades exploring why people repeat patterns, override intuition, and abandon themselves in the name of love.

In ***Stop Dating Red Flags***, Karen turns that lens inward. What began as a brutally honest look at her own relationship history became a guide for women ready to break cycles, rebuild self-trust, and stop negotiating their worth.

Karen is also the author of several books exploring consciousness, creativity, and human awareness. Across all her work, one theme remains constant: personal responsibility is power.

She writes the way she lives—honest, bold, and grounded in truth. Karen lives in the beautiful desert of Arizona, where she continues writing, teaching, dancing, and reminding women to keep their crown on.

Learn more at: **creativevisionspublications.com/redflags**

Your words help other women recognize the red flags sooner.
I'd truly appreciate you sharing your thoughts in a review.

Scan to leave a review.

Ready to do the work?

Stop Dating Red Flags: The Action Plan Workbook takes you beyond awareness and into action.

It's designed to help you recognize your patterns, rebuild self-trust, and start choosing yourself differently.

Scan to get the workbook.